The School of Hard Knocks

10 Lessons To Help You Succeed In Life

Published in the United States by:

Eternal Three Publishing, LLC
P.O. Box 658
Wylie, TX 75098

www.eternal3.com

Book Editor: Tim Munday

Crest Design and Pictures: Sonia Cristales for Visual Narratives

Book Cover Design: A.C. Cristales with assistance provided by Genesis Productions,
www.genesisproductions.net

Disclaimer and Authors' Note

The authors and publisher shall have neither liability or responsibility to anyone with respect to any loss or damage caused, or alleged to be caused, directly or indirectly by the information contained in this book.

This is a work of nonfiction. We have rendered the events faithfully and truthfully just as we have recalled them. Some names and descriptions of individuals have been changed in order to respect their privacy. To anyone whose name we did not recall or omitted, we offer sincere apologies. While circumstance and conversations depicted herein come from our keen recollection of them, they are not meant to represent exact word-for-word reenactments of our life. They are told in a way that evokes the real feeling and meaning of what was said and our view of what happened to us, in keeping with the true essence of the mood and spirit of those moments that shaped our life.

ISBN-13: 978-0692266625

ISBN-10: 0692266623

To our mother, Nati Cristales, our greatest teacher

You take our hand, expand our minds, and inspire our hearts.

To our children, AJ, Aliyah, Isabella, our reasons "why"

We hope to do for you what your grandmother does for us.

To all who never stop believing in us, thank you.

Faith, Hope, Love. Eternally.

Course Catalogue

Introduction

My brother and I served as administrators in the public school system for a number of years. Whether as teachers, mentors, disciplinarians, or simply friends, we saw reflections of ourselves in the students we supervised every day. As they walked the hallways or sat in our offices, we saw young men and women who were happy, confident, triumphant, alive. In equal measure, we also saw those who were discouraged, afraid, lost, and beaten.

We were no different when we called school our home; we, too, walked on both sides of the emotional spectrum. We are no different now. Save that we are a little older, a little bit wiser, we still ride the same roller coaster created by our experiences in this life. Over the years, we have learned to sit back and enjoy the peaks and valleys of this ride because we know we only get to take part in it one time. Just as importantly, we have also learned to rely upon three eternal principles to guide us—faith, hope, and love.

The foundation of this book and its lessons come from these three principles incubated in the hardships and heartaches of two Hispanic boys who, in the midst of their trials, always believed they would come out on top. It was this belief that we worked to instill in the young men and women we served as members of the school system, and it is this same belief that we wish to instill in others today. You see, our journey is not yet complete. There is still more for us to do, more mountains to climb, more summits to reach. This is why we decided to resign from our jobs as administrators and pursue our dreams of speaking and writing to men and women such as yourselves. Now our purpose is bigger . . .

Our purpose is to reach the world.

You may wonder what qualifies us for such an undertaking, and that would be a fair question to ask. Growing up we cussed out teachers and befriended the wrong kinds of people. We took the road most traveled because it was easy. We were foolish, and people rightly called us fools because of this. Alone, the decisions to do these things hardly grant us much credibility. However, despite having made such choices, my brother and I still emerged as college graduates, both receiving not only our Bachelor's degrees, but our Master's degrees as well. We evolved from students into teachers, and from teachers into principals. The trials of life weakened us at times, but because we weathered them, we were able to help encourage in others the same strength they imparted to us. Little did we know that two pint-sized hellraisers in school would one day become trailblazers, first in the lives of our students and today in the lives of so many others.

But our greatest sense of accomplishment has never been in what we have attained. Rather, it has been in what we have overcome. One of our harshest memories is that of seeing our mother being verbally and physically abused. Anyone who has been forced to witness this in his or her own life knows how devastating such a sight can be. Despite this, however, great memories were also born, the memories of two young boys who would hop into their mother's beat-up Corolla right after school and travel throughout Dallas to office buildings and daycare centers, sweeping and cleaning their way through life. It has been a life of hardships to be sure, one that is still playing itself out as we continue striving for greatness. But like the old saying goes, "Without struggle, there can be no progress."

We both would agree that while our shared moments of laughter have brought us closer together, it is the tears we have cried on one another's shoulders that have bound us for life. In our seventy-eight combined years of living, we have been through many things. No two seasons have ever been the same. We have experienced the frigidity of loneliness in juxtaposition to the warmth of togetherness. We have survived the storms of uncertainty, but we have also lived through the peace of purpose. Family members and so-called friends have said they loved us one day only to curse us with their words and looks the next. Opportunities have been found, others taken for granted, and still others lost. But, through it all, we have learned to survive, to overcome, to rise above adversity. Through it all, even amidst the shadows of change, we have been like two trees planted along the riverbank, enduring the heat, overcoming the drought, and still bearing fruit. We have never surrendered the hope of fulfilling our dreams.

Every person chases after something. So often those who are running are judged by where they are in the race or, sadly, by onlookers' perceptions of where the finish line lies even while the contest continues.

One lesson we have learned, however, is that how a person comes out of the gates when the gun goes off is less important than if he or she finishes the race. Along the way, we all will do foolish things that will cause us to stumble, and many people will want to dismiss our participation outright because of this. Life will occasionally weaken us to the point that we will want to give up on all that we have set our hearts and minds to do. Failures will humble us, perhaps so much that we will feel as though we are nobodies. But like the song we sang back in Sunday school says, "Nobody's a nobody. Everybody is somebody."

Especially you.

Because of faith, hope, and love we have committed ourselves to staying loyal to who we are and what we have set out to do. The lessons you are about to read are the truths we have discovered along our path toward finding success and purpose in our own lives. They have set us free. May they do the same for you.

Eternal 3.

A.C. and Axel Cristales

Orientation

Congratulations!

You have been selected for admission into a school of higher learning, a school unlike any other you have attended or even heard of in the past. Enrollment here is not contingent upon entrance exams, an application process, or even tuition, but rather your desire to grow beyond the man or woman you are and to experience life in a richer and more meaningful way. Our professors do not care who you are, how much money and power you may have, or how much you may lack. Here, every heart and mind will have the opportunity to expand, every learner will be granted the same degree of respect and held to the same standards and expectations. In our classrooms and lecture halls, you will sit alongside both the young and old. Throughout our hallways, you will rub elbows with people from all over the world and from all walks of life. Some of you will crawl while others may run, but ultimately you will all work toward the same goal—maturity and freedom gained through an honest evaluation of your experiences, failures and victories alike.

You must enter this school knowing that you will never again be the same. Your preconceived notions of what is true and what is false will be stripped away. If you are proud, you will be humbled; if you are humble, you will be made powerful. If you are dedicated, you will thrive; if you grow faint, you may need to repeat your courses or risk being left behind. You will graduate only once you have learned to become greater than your challenges, so prepare yourself now.

Welcome to the School of Hard Knocks.

Opportunity 101

Course Description

Everyone is given chances to make a positive impact in life. Each day brings with it new opportunities to make the world a better place, both for ourselves and for others. In order to do this, however, we must first learn how to recognize our potential and live up to it, even amidst our difficulties.

Being aware of the opportunities that surround you, believing in yourself enough to make the most of them, and working tirelessly to see the culmination of your efforts are essential to success in this course, in those that follow, and in life. Will you choose to seize the opportunities set before you and let them carry you toward something greater, or will you instead choose to let them slip through your fingers? Destiny awaits your decision.

We sit. We wait. We hope.

But exactly what do we sit and wait and hope for? If you asked one hundred different people that question, chances are you would receive one hundred different answers, and the majority would be excuses meant to hide one unfortunate truth—for many people, it is easier to be complacent and simply accept their circumstances than to show initiative, take action, and improve them.

In our experience, the people who have adopted this mindset seem to believe that opportunities fall from the sky like golden apples just waiting to be discovered. They sit anticipating that "aha" moment when the possibility of doing something significant finally reveals itself. Inwardly, however, they do not believe this will ever really happen, at least not to them. After all, *real* opportunities only present themselves to others. So they remain idle, hope constantly fading as each day blends into the next with no change in sight. In all their waiting, their lives become one long stretch of night with only brief periods of sunlight.

The reality is that we are constantly being presented with opportunities to do something worthwhile with our lives. Most people do not realize this, but every day, from the moment we wake up until the moment we lay down to rest, we have the potential to change the world. Yes, the very fact that you have been blessed with another day is proof enough that you have been summoned to do something great. Why else would you still be here if not to seek out chances to make a difference in your life and in the lives of those around you? If you are one of those just sitting passively waiting for a sign that your time to act has finally arrived, we have news for you. Despite what the old adage says, opportunity does not always knock. And even when it does, there is no guarantee that we will recognize it.

There are many reasons for this. As we get older, our days seem to become shorter than they once were. Our responsibilities consume so much of our time and energy, on occasion there simply are not enough hours in the day to attend to them all. If we focus too intently on these activities, we can easily miss others that do not fit into our established routines. At other times, we may ignore things outside the realm of what we find comfortable, choosing instead to maintain the status quo because we do not want to disrupt the practices we have become accustomed to. At still other times, we may fail to recognize the opportunities that arise because they do not come in the manner we expect or because, on the surface, they look far too much like work. It is possible for us to spend so much time in expectation and preparation for what may come that we actually miss the very things we are waiting for until they have passed well beyond our grasp. Regardless of the reason, the truth is that far too often we allow opportunities to remain unclaimed when they should, in fact, be fortuitously seized.

We are men who have experienced both sides of this issue. For as much as we may take hold of them now, there have been times in our lives when we have failed to see our own opportunities because we were too preoccupied with other things or other people.

"As a freshman, instead of taking advantage of the gift that I had been given as the first person in my family to be accepted into college, I got caught up with some friends who introduced me to the wild side of campus life. Instead of losing myself in my books and studying, I lost myself to partying and drinking, and this led to me being put on academic probation.

"I remember making the four-hour drive home from Houston to Dallas after this

thinking the entire time, *'What am I going to tell Mom?'* I had wasted my time in school and was ashamed. I felt like I had spat on my mother's hard-earned money and years of hard work, as well as disregarded the example of dedication and commitment she had set for me. I came back home with my tail tucked between my legs.

"I realized I had made a mistake and that it was going to require no small amount of work on my behalf to get back on track. But I kept my purpose in mind: success and nothing less. Refusing to give up or give in, I started all over again, enrolling at a local community college. I continued my education at this level for a year and half. When my grades were acceptable, I transferred back to a four-year university, once again on my way toward earning my Bachelor's degree. It took me four and half years to finally receive it, but I did it.

"The beginning of my college life threw me several curve balls, many of which I swung at and missed and some of which knocked me down. But each time I got up, dusted myself off, got back into the batter's box, and continued swinging away. I knew if I just kept at it, second chances would open up for me. I also knew that when they did, I would have two choices: either to take them on or allow them to pass me by. I resolved to do the former, and I learned a valuable lesson in doing so—when difficult situations are mastered, opportunities are also won."

- Axel Cristales

We only progress in our lives when we seize the chances we are presented. If we permit our spirits to be weakened by initial failures, we allow those chances to slip away and, in the wake of their passing, allow bitterness over our loss to creep into our hearts as well. Once this happens, complaints about the unfairness of life are sure to follow.

We certainly have not been immune to this in the past. We were once very immature and believed the world should have conformed itself to our desires. During this phase, we did little else but complain about a litany of perceived injustices, blind to reality the entire time. We complained about not growing up in a perfect family, all the while failing to recognize that no family is perfect. We complained about the difficulties associated with growing up without a real father, living in lower-middle class society, and receiving good shoes and gear only on our birthdays and, if we were good, for Christmas. The one thing we failed to consider through all of our groaning was that there were others suffering through even greater disadvantages than we were facing, many of whom were doing more with less and were doing so without grumbling. Lord Jeffrey of Amherst, a general of the British forces during the French and Indian War, once said, "The tendency to whining and complaining may be taken as the surest sign, and symptom, of little souls and inferior intellects." At that point in our lives, those words described us fairly well.

We believe there are three dangers inherent to complaining:

1. *People will not want to associate with you.*

    No one wants to affiliate themselves with those who only respond negatively to the challenges they face. Such people can neither be encouraged nor bring encouragement to others. They are unlikely to be considered candidates for advancement in the workplace or elsewhere. Those who only utter grievances fail to inspire either confidence or goodwill in those around them. Perhaps you are a loner and having people around you is the last thing you concern yourself with, but you would do well to remember that it is our relationships with people that open doors for us.

2. *Complaining will ruin your day . . . and perhaps even your life.*

    The more we focus on something, the greater its ability to influence our lives becomes. As human beings, we have a natural tendency to gravitate toward the negative. (If you need proof of this, ask the next person you see about his or her day and listen carefully to the first things he or she shares.) This is why it is imperative that you watch what you say and do. The more you focus on what may be going wrong or on what you may lack, the more prone you are to discouragement and the more likely you are to become a source of discouragement for others.

3. *Complaining stunts your growth.*

There are two types of people in life—spectators and participants. Spectators get as close as possible to the events going on around them without ever actually taking part in them. Participants, by contrast, live to get involved in the action. The thrill for spectators comes only from sitting, observing, and criticizing, but participants experience the joy of victory firsthand. For them, even the agony of defeat is a reward because failures demonstrate areas in which they can improve, areas in which they can grow. Win or lose, they gain valuable experience no one can ever take away from them. You must decide for yourself which type of person you will be. The benefits or consequences of that decision rest on your shoulders alone.

Complaining will not make you better. It will only make you bitter. Take a moment to honestly evaluate your situation. If you find yourself in a position where grievances dominate your thoughts and poison your words, we would like to remind you that even though you may not have an immediate opportunity to change your circumstances, you *always* have the ability to change your attitude. Improve your situation through the gift of perspective. You are much bigger than any problem you may be facing, your spirit much stronger. Opportunities lie and wait, ready for you to claim them. Visualize yourself in a position of power taking the necessary steps to reach them, overcoming whatever obstacles you must, then make that vision a reality. Improve your outlook, and you will improve your entire life as well.

We should warn you, of course, that you must be on guard against anything which may attempt to steer you from your purpose. Be aware that unexpected events may threaten your enthusiasm. You must not let them do so.

"It is easy to see opportunities in good times, but doing so during those moments when you feel that you will never make it is another story entirely.

"I worked hard to graduate from high school in three years, and I was well rewarded for my efforts. The State of Texas gave me one thousand dollars for graduating early, money I was able to put to excellent use in my pursuit of higher education. During my time in community college, I was also afforded the chance to work as a bilingual teacher's aide for a local school district. The school district, in turn, paid for my college tuition and textbooks. These

were great opportunities that I recognized immediately. Others, those that came during more difficult times, were harder to distinguish, but fortunately I was able to identify and take hold of them as well.

"In late May of 1999, I was set to graduate from South Garland High School. It was a joyous moment for me because several of the friends I had grown up with did not reach this benchmark. It was also a moment of great pride, namely because my parents only made it to fifth grade. People who knew what type of man my father was had predicted that I would follow in his footsteps. In their eyes, there was no way that I was going to graduate from high school, much less become a leader in education. But at seventeen years old, I was about to walk across the stage and receive a diploma that neither my father nor my mother ever had a chance of receiving.

"As I was walking out to the car, I saw my father standing there. Since he had abandoned us years before, his appearance was surprising to say the least. I do not know if he was high on drugs, but he was acting very peculiar. What transpired was something that has stayed with me ever since.

"My father badly wanted to speak to my mom. I knew by his tone that whatever he was going to say to her was not going to be good, so I asked him what he wanted. He said very sternly, 'Just let me talk to your mom.' Naturally feeling very protective of her, I said, 'No! You're not going to talk her like that.' That angered him, and he went on a tirade, cursing in Spanish and telling us that we had to come up with $10,000 or he was going kick us out of the house we were living in.

"That experience was one for the ages. There was no, 'Hey, son. I'm proud of

29

you. You are about to graduate and you are doing it in three years. How great is that!' No, instead it was, 'I need your mom to give me $10,000, or I'm kicking you guys out of this house.'

"My mother, brother, and I couldn't believe what we were hearing. To have my father come on a day that was meant to be special and not care about it upset me. As I watched my father get into his car and speed off, I realized that I had a decision to make, the outcome of which was going to affect me not only on my graduation day, but also for the rest of my life—I could respond in anger or I could bring something good out of my misfortune. I made the smart choice. My father may have missed an opportunity to be proud, but not me.

"I can honestly say that although I was hurt by my father's actions that day, I attended my high school graduation and had a wonderful time. I remember giving my mother a huge hug and letting her know that I wasn't finished. There was more for me to accomplish and even without the support of my father, I was going to succeed.

"I could have squandered the opportunity to find the silver lining in that dark cloud and allowed the situation with my father to deter me from my purpose. Instead, I chose to remain positive. We may not be able to control how others act toward us, but we *can* control how we respond to them. Every waking moment provides us with opportunities to do this in a positive manner. We should make the most of them and do just that."

- A.C. Cristales

As we prepare to bring this first course to a close, please allow us to share a story about making the best of what you are given.

There once was a rich CEO who was going on an extended vacation to the Bahamas. Before leaving, he called a meeting with three of his managers to delegate the responsibilities each would have in his absence.

The CEO distributed accounts to each of these managers, accounts that varied in value according to their abilities. To the first, he gave five thousand dollars; to the second, two thousand dollars; and to the third, one thousand dollars. Once this task was completed, he left for his vacation.

The manager who had been given five thousand dollars quickly went to work and doubled his boss's investment. The second manager followed suit and achieved the same result. The third manager, however, deposited the money placed in his care but did nothing more.

Several months later, the CEO returned from his vacation and again had a meeting with his managers. The manager given five thousand dollars showed him how he had doubled his investment. The CEO commended him, saying, "Excellent work! You were faithful with the little I gave you. Now I know I can trust you with much more."

The manager given two thousand dollars also showed the CEO how he doubled his investment. The CEO commended him as well, saying once again, "Excellent work! You were faithful with the little I gave you. Now I know I can trust you with much more."

The manager given one thousand dollars said, "Sir, I know that you have high standards for your company and dislike those who act carelessly. I also know that you demand the best and have very little patience for error. So I deposited your investment in the bank where I would not lose it and therefore disappoint you. Here is your money, safe and secure to the last penny."

The CEO was furious. To the third manager he said, "That is a terrible way to live. In fact, it is *deplorable to live so cautiously! If you truly knew I was after the best, why then did you not do your best with what I gave you? The least you could have done was invest this amount in a three-month CD and allow it to accumulate interest. Yet you didn't even do that. Son, you no longer work for my company. I cannot have someone who plays it safe and is afraid to go out and work with what I give him."*

Blood, sweat, and tears have gone into the writing of this book, all in the hopes of accomplishing greater things in our lives. We have faced challenges in the past, and we continue to face challenges today in pursuit of our goal. Should we succeed or should we fail in the future, at least we will know that we have tried, that we have put everything into fulfilling our dreams and have left nothing on the field. We have made difficult decisions in order to seize the opportunities set before us, decisions others have questioned the wisdom of. But we are certain that we are on the right path, and we are stepping out on faith in order to follow it to its conclusion.

You are no different than us. We all have the potential to do something significant, something that will make a lasting impact on the world. We all face difficulties, some of which may seem overwhelming. But within each one of us is the strength to overcome hardship if only we can accept the fact that great opportunities sometimes camouflage themselves in impossible situations.

Be strong and courageous, for it is the resolute and the brave who tear down the obstacles before them and make opportunities for themselves where seemingly none exist. Do not be merely a spectator. Pursue your dreams, and if you get knocked down one hundred times, get up one hundred and one. Endure the pain, endure the uncertainty . . . and do so without complaining.

And remember, life is not about getting the best cards. It is about playing the cards you are dealt, knowing that, at some point, you will have to go all in. Be faithful with what you have been given, even if it is only a little, and in time you will gain much more.

Do not hesitate. The time to set about conquering the day begins the minute your feet hit the floor.

Your time to act is now.

Opportunity 101
Questions for Reflection

1. Identify at least three instances in which you allowed opportunities to slip away from you. Why do you think you let this happen? In what ways would your life be different had you taken hold of them?

2. They say opportunity only knocks once. What steps can you take to better ensure that you will be able to hear it when it does? Do you recognize the need to change anything in your life in order for this to be possible? What are they and how will you implement them?

3. The actions you take today will directly affect everything else that occurs around you. Identify at least three things you can do that will make an impact in your life and in the lives of others close to you. How will you go about creating the opportunity to put these things into immediate action? Once you have decided how you will do this, do not hesitate to put your plans into effect.

4. Remember, "Complaining will not make you better. It will only make you bitter." When you feel yourself grumbling, what is a more personal axiom you can recite? Write this down, post it in prominent places, and repeat it whenever necessary.

5. If you knew you were going to die within the next six months, what opportunities would you seize without thinking twice? Can any of these things be pursued now? If so, begin looking into them and laying out plans to make them happen.

Challenges 101

Course Description

Say whatever we will, there is no denying the fact that life can be difficult. Challenges emerge from unexpected sources at unforeseen times; they cannot be avoided, nor can they long be ignored. Confronting them can be trying, but allowing them to linger only permits the pain they can inflict to linger as well.

You must accept life for what it is. Learn to withstand your challenges, and you will foster a maturity of spirit unattainable by any other means. Will you attempt to hide from the trials in your life and allow them to continue exerting influence over you, or will you embrace the process of confronting them and, in turn, give your life deeper meaning?

"Embrace the Struggle," one of the primary principles of the *Eternal 3* program, deals with the acceptance of challenges. The core beliefs behind this principle are:

- Challenges are inevitably going to come our way;

- Trying to avoid challenges is an exercise in futility, therefore we should instead focus our time and energy on how we will manage them;

- If we embrace the uncomfortable aspects of our lives, we can later use them as tools for growth.

At its heart, this issue centers on one vital question—will we grant our trials power over us by facing them with uncertainty, timidity, and fear, or will we appropriate that power for ourselves by refusing to back down no matter how difficult they may be? The answer to this question is of vital importance as it has a direct impact on the course our lives will take.

My brother and I have chosen to do the latter. We have made this decision, in part, because experience has taught us the wisdom in doing so. As we touched on above, we have learned that our trials can actually be used as springboards for positive transformation. But there is also a very practical reason behind this decision. We embrace our challenges because, in reality, we can do nothing else. No matter where we turn, challenges await us. They are simply a part of life. Frank Sinatra understood this. He touched upon it in a song appropriately titled, "That's Life" . . . and no one sings it better than the "Chairman of the Board."

"That's life.
That's what all the people say.
You're riding high in April, shot down in May.
But I know I'm gonna change that tune.
When I'm back on top, back on top in June."

Consider all the difficulties that confront society today: poverty, crime, divorce, single-parent homes, physical and mental disabilities, bullying . . . the list goes on and on. Challenges are everywhere, and we must meet them head on or else fail in everything we set out to do. It is that simple. Bette Davis touched on this best when she said, "The key to life is accepting challenges. Once someone stops doing this, he's dead."

We are not suggesting this will always be easy. It very rarely is. In fact, when challenges come our way, the easy response is to give way to self-pity and ask ourselves, "Why did this happen to me?" We may ask this question repeatedly when facing hardships, and it will weigh us down if we allow it because only seldom do we find the answer. In reality, however, the "why" behind our challenges is less important than the "what," namely "What will I do when they arise?" and "What will I take away from my experiences so they will not seem so overwhelming when I encounter similar circumstances in the future?" If we live long enough and face enough difficulties in this manner, we can not only learn how to grow through them, but perhaps learn how to embrace them as well.

"I can honestly say that I have confronted challenges my entire life. I can recall a conversation I had with my mother a few years ago when I was working on a sociology project for a class that centered on marriage and family. I asked her if she and my father planned on having me. She quickly responded, 'No.' My first challenge, then—being unwanted from conception—rose against me even before I was born.

"There were other challenges that I had to face at an early stage in my life as well. On several occasions, my brother has told me about the many times my dad would physically abuse my mother while she was pregnant with me. My mother has shared more specific details about this, including the time he tried to push her out of the car while it was still moving! I faced hurdle after hurdle, and I hadn't even breathed the air in Texas nor had anyone ever seen my beautiful newborn face or head full of dark hair.

"Some would make the case that my mom was the main recipient of my father's mistreatment, and rightfully so. However, there is no denying the fact that what affected my mom also affected me as I grew inside of her. Before I had even entered this world, I faced seemingly insurmountable odds. Many times I have asked myself why I had to endure these trials. Were they meant to make me stronger? Were they meant to

test my spirit and determine if I had the character to pursue the things that I really wanted in life? My daughter just turned five, and I do not remember her wanting anything more than rest and her *leche* (milk) when she was a baby. She didn't need to be strengthened or tested. Why did I?"

- A.C. Cristales

We can pretend all we want that challenges do not exist, but that does not make them any less real. They present themselves when we least expect them, and even when we see them coming, they often still hit us harder than we anticipate they will. They stretch us only to stretch us more. They beat us only to beat us again. At times it may seem as if they stand over us, laughing at our inability to conquer them. Understand, then, that this life will either make or break us depending on how we respond to the hardships that come our way.

"I was bullied as a child. Mom left for work at daybreak. The bus picked my

brother up and took him to his school on the other side of town. That meant I had to walk five blocks to and from school alone every day. I dreaded walking out of the house and making that five-block trek to school because I knew I was going to encounter the two punks who got their kicks tormenting me.

"They hated on me simply because I was a high-achieving Hispanic in a school where students were separated into general- and bilingual-education classrooms. Because I had picked up the English language more quickly than the other Hispanics in my grade level, I was exited out of the bilingual class and put with the *gringos* my third-grade year. I didn't know this would make me a sell-out, an outcast among my own kind. Jealousy and envy have a way of devaluing your worth, and that was exactly what these two non-English speaking knuckleheads were trying to do to me. It was a tough and confusing time to say the least.

"I can still remember the Spanish cuss words they would yell at me before pushing me to the ground. I would like to say that I sought help and stood up to them, that they didn't find me after I changed the direction I walked to school. No such luck. It wasn't until these two brothers eventually moved out of the neighborhood that I was finally left alone.

"Frustrating though they were at the time, I can look back at those encounters now and take three things from them. First, the higher we climb, the greater the number of people who will try to drag us back down again. Second, challenges strengthen the mind in much the same way that hard work strengthens the body. Third, while challenges in life are inevitable, being defeated is a choice.

"It's strange to me how life tends to follow a circular path. As the principal of an elementary school, one of my duties was to deal with bullies. If it was a legitimate case of bullying, I dealt with the situation accordingly whether it required a harsh conversation, suspension, or even moving one of the students to another school. I did this because just like I needed someone in my corner, the bullied kids also needed someone in theirs."

- Axel Cristales

The troubles that seem overwhelming in our lives are usually made up of many smaller problems. We have to be willing to take on these smaller problems, or we will be crushed beneath their collective weight. Because smaller issues can be tackled individually, they can be conquered far more easily. With each victory we gain, the perceived behemoth we are struggling against becomes weaker. In time, as we continue to whittle away at its foundation, it will fall to pieces entirely. As my brother and I have learned, understanding this simple principle is essential to survival against adversity.

We could have thrown in the towel a long time ago. We could have allowed the challenges in our lives to sound the death knell of our dreams, but we choose another path. It was not always easy, and it was rarely fun. We took many beatings, emotional and physical, before we were finally willing to stand up and say, "No more!" Once we did, however, we became warriors, directly confronting whatever challenges arose, one by one. Sometimes we won, sometimes we lost; sometimes we laughed, sometimes we cried . . . but we never allowed the troubles that came against us to drive us to the point where we were willing to give up our hopes and dreams. Instead, we hung in there because we knew difficulties, much like storms, eventually pass on. Challenges do not last forever. Neither should their effects on our lives.

Life is what it is, but it is also what we choose to make of it. As long as you still draw breath, as long as you are alive, you still have the opportunity to conquer the challenges facing you and revel in the sense of triumph found therein. You still have the opportunity to set and achieve your goals.

One of our greatest achievements in life was completing the "Soldier Field Run," a ten-mile run that ended at the 50-yard line of Soldier Field in Chicago. Up to that time, neither of us could remember ever having run more than two miles, so ten miles seemed daunting. But we had committed ourselves to the task, and we were not going to back down.

When the gun sounded and we set out, we were able to maintain a steady pace that was not too taxing. We passed the two-mile marker fine, still breathing lightly. At three miles, however, our minds started playing tricks on us. At mile four, our legs began feeling heavier, as if we were each dragging two flat tires. Our lungs felt like land mines prepared to detonate at any misstep, but we pressed on. When we got to mile five, we looked at one another and knew that if we had gotten that far we could make it the rest of the way. What our bodies were telling us was irrelevant because in our minds we both kept hearing the same question . . .

"*How bad do you want it?*"

The last four miles we ran together, encouraging one another every tiring step of the way.

We saw people on the side of the trail doubled over in pain from the cramps that had overtaken them, stopping them short of their goal. The closer we got to the end, the more pressing became the possibility that the same would happen to us. But we wanted to cross that finish line inside the stadium of our beloved Chicago Bears badly enough to refuse succumbing to them. We completed our run, and we did so with our hands held high in triumph.

Has there ever been a moment in your life when you have felt something similar? Ponder that question for a moment. If you can answer it in the affirmative, we have another for you to consider as well. Did these feelings develop when times were easy or when you accomplished something difficult, something worthwhile, something you felt was going to break you but did not?

Some people will stop halfway to their finish line and allow themselves to be defeated by the belief that the challenge is far greater than the glory. Of course there will be difficulties when someone is seeking to reach a mountaintop, but there will be difficulties for those who choose to remain in the valley as well. At least those striving for greatness have the hope of reward for having endured them.

Challenges exist for a reason, and that reason is *not* to keep you from what you want to achieve. They exist to reveal how much you want something, to determine whether or not you want it badly enough to endure whatever it takes to earn it.

If you have goals in life, you will have to face adversity in order to reach them. If you have dreams, you will have to endure struggles in order to see them come to fruition. Such things are essential for growth. Trials are meant to be tough because it is during the tough moments that we find out what we are made of. It is our times of hardship that truly reveal what is within us. Periods of ease and leisure alone will never prepare us for the trials looming just beyond our sight. We become tough only by going through tough times.

Do not handicap yourself or your future by seeking to make your life easier. We know it is difficult to look adversity in the eye and smile, but we encourage you to do just that. Learn to consider challenges as opportunities in disguise. Face them, even if they seem impossible; embrace them and build yourself up. Attempt even the most difficult things. You can only grow stronger from the experience. You must be willing to face to the difficulties that come your way, and you must learn to use them as springboards for growth. This will not happen without your conscious and concerted effort. Unlike passing from childhood into adolescence, this must be intentional.

We understand that this will not be easy. We have certainly had days when we woke up and, even though the sun had risen and shone through our windows, we could not see it because the shadow cast by the difficulties we were facing loomed far too largely. In those moments, life seemed bleak, and our visions for the future were blurred. In the darkness, even we found ourselves believing there was no hope. Amidst those temporary lapses, however, our belief that the grandest things lay just on the other side of our tribulations urged us to hold on.

Take a moment to reflect upon some of the things that never would have existed had their creators allowed challenges to derail them from their destinies.

Today, Ludwig van Beethoven is regarded as one of the greatest composers who ever lived. Although he went completely deaf at the height of his career, he still created the beautiful music he is remembered for, and this without the use of his most important sense. Had he allowed adversity to stop him, we would not have the expressive and artistic pieces he composed, music still admired and performed after two hundred years.

Alexander Graham Bell, as we all know, was one of the originators of the first telephone. What many people are not aware of, however, is the fact that he set about creating this device in order to overcome the challenges inherent to communicating with his deaf wife. It was his love for her that motivated him to turn an obstacle into an opportunity. We now have the ability to carry phones on our wrists, all due to the humble beginnings of this invention.

We will speak more on persistence later, but for now we will simply ask you to imagine the books and songs that never would have been written, the ideas and inventions that never would have seen the light of day if their creators had allowed temporary failure to fester into permanent defeat.

Remember, as long as you have air in your lungs and your heart still beats, hope still lives inside you. It is up to you to breathe life into it. Yes, you will face challenges, but you do not have to succumb to them. Rise above them. Do not be afraid.

As we draw this course to a close, again we would like to leave you with a story.

Two friends were walking along a dark and desolate valley. Each was desperate to find a new and better life, but to that point their journey had failed to offer either man any hope.

One day they arrived at the base of a breathtaking, but tall and rugged mountain. At its crown was a beautiful, snowcapped peak. Both friends stopped in their tracks and stared in awe.

One of the men said aloud, "That's a beautiful mountaintop."

The other responded with but a single word, "And?"

The first man replied, "No, no. You don't get it. I see the mountaintop."

Again the other responded with a single word, this time spoken with greater agitation, "And?"

The first man said, "I want to reach that mountaintop. I want to get there." The other could only see the challenges such an effort would present.

"Do you know how difficult it would be to climb up there? It has to be nearly 18,000 feet high. It's impossible. You can't do it."

The first man calmly addressed his friend saying, "That is precisely why I will. You see, challenges were never meant to stop us, but to encourage us to work toward greater things. I don't know about you, but I am going to the top."

At this the two men parted ways, the first pressing on toward his goal while the other remained motionless, silently watching as his friend disappeared in the distance.

Are you currently experiencing trials? Are you presently struggling to overcome difficulties? Perhaps the challenges in your life are causing you to question your decision to pursue your dreams. Perhaps they have caused you suffering or forced you to sacrifice things you value, like the security of your home or family or friends. Take heart. You do not have to bow before them.

Whatever you may be facing, do not let the fear of what lies ahead of you chase away the faith that has followed you, pushing you along. Great difficulties must bring about even greater strength of heart. There can be no turning back. Find the courage to maintain your conviction, to remain firm in your purpose. Embrace your challenges. Endure your battles. Do not allow present troubles to rob you of future glories. Use them instead as stepping stones toward your destiny.

Above all, resolve to give it everything you have, to remain on the battlefield until the final victory is won. We are here to tell that not only *can* you make it, but also that you *will* make it if only you refuse to give in.

Do not allow challenges to keep you rooted in the valleys of life. Press on toward your own mountaintop, no matter how difficult the journey may appear to be. You *can* overcome the obstacles in your life.

We believe in you.

Challenges 101
Questions for Reflection

1. Sometimes we are blindsided by unexpected difficulties in life. When we find ourselves in such a predicament, what is the first thing a person should do? Explain why you believe this response is the correct one to make.

2. Describe a moment in your life when you chose to confront a challenge head on. How did you approach it? What actions did you take to overcome it? Were they successful? Unsuccessful? Regardless of the outcome, what did you learn from the experience?

3. It is easy to get caught up in the *why* of "Why did this happen to me?" However, as discussed in this course, the *what* of "What will I do when challenges arise?" is actually far more important. Explain why focusing on *what* you will do when confronted with a challenge is more important than *why* you are facing it.

4. We have all been defeated by challenges at one time or another in our lives. We have all likewise overcome them. Compare a time when you were defeated and a time when you were victorious. How did you approach them differently? Why were you more successful in one situation than the other?

5. What mountaintop do you desire to reach? What are some difficulties you believe you will face on your journey? As things currently stand, do you feel that you are strong enough to conquer them and, if so, how will you go about doing so? If not, what can you do now to prepare yourself for the challenges you predict you will encounter?

Opposition 101

Course Description

The dreamer, the believer, the seeker, the doer all have one thing in common— each of them faces opposition. The spirit that inspires our dreams, the certainty that establishes our beliefs, the inspiration that shapes our visions, and the purpose that guides our actions will, at some point, be attacked by naysayers. Whether through criticism, rejection, intimidation, or even hatred, such people will always attempt to infect us with just enough self-doubt and insecurity to sway us from achieving our goals.

True success comes not from what you achieve, but rather from what you overcome. Opposition will not kill you, but it *will* strengthen you if properly faced and addressed. Will you resolve to silence antagonistic voices through faith and do what they say cannot be done, or will you choose to yield to them and thereby prove them correct?

Opposition comes in many forms through many voices . . .

"You can't do that. You don't have the talent."

"That's not good enough. I could have done it better."

"You're not what we're looking for."

Webster's dictionary defines opposition as, "An action that is done to stop or defeat someone or something." While this definition is certainly adequate, we prefer the way Sir Isaac Newton described this concept while explaining his third law of motion: "For every action there is an equal and opposite reaction." As we apply this law to the subject at hand, we interpret it to mean that for every optimist encouraging us on to greater heights, there will also be a pessimist desiring to hold us back; for every dream being pursued, there will also be a monster intent on stopping us short of success. In short, as we attempt to move forward in our lives, we *will* face opposition.

More often than not, the resistance we face comes from uninspired thinkers. Perhaps Albert Einstein said it best when he wrote, "Great spirits have always encountered violent opposition from mediocre minds." The greatest problem with "mediocre minds" as he referred to them, is that they suffer from tunnel vision. What lies beyond their own narrow perspective they discount or ignore. They see greatness as being intended only for the select few, and this distorts their belief system accordingly. If we have little as children, they believe we should be prepared to have little as adults as well. They feel that the mistakes of our parents will be repeated in our lives, that cycles of failure cannot be broken, that the world needs more ditch-diggers and bricklayers than it does destiny-seekers and dreamchasers. They believe these things because they have not achieved anything noteworthy in their own lives, therefore no one else should be allowed to either.

"I remember when I became a principal. There were people close to me, family members, who started belittling my success, mockingly saying things such as, 'Must be nice to sit in an office all day, not doing anything except propping your feet up on the desk.' and 'How hard a job can it be when you have summers off?'

"What I've learned is that small-minded people not only lack sense, they also lack

perspective. They see the result, but they fail to see the process that made it possible. Yes, it was nice to sit an office and be the chief decision-maker in the school. It was also nice having six weeks off during the summers to enjoy time with my children. But it was also very hard work having two (and sometimes three) jobs my last two years in college; it was tiring staying up sleepless nights to study for tests I knew I would barely pass; it was stressful driving one hundred miles a day from school to job to job in a beat-up car with no A/C in the hot Texas summers, wondering the entire time if the motor was going to give out.

"I'll never apologize for my success. I've attained what I've attained because I was willing to go through the process required to earn it. I am who I am because I understood that hard work, and even the criticism it spawned from

others, would all become part of my makeup."

Do not give the shortsightedness and self-doubt of other people authority over you. Do not allow your dreams to die or your destiny to be delayed. Do not permit yourself to be knocked off course. Stand firm and encourage yourself when necessary. Even if one door closes, others will remain open and allow you to continue on toward your purpose.

You have the ability to make your life better. You have gifts that are meant to be shared, meant to be used to help those around you. You have a vision, perhaps still waiting to be discovered, that must be pursued not only for your benefit, but also for the benefit of the world. You have dreams that may very well change the course of history.

This is why you face opposition. You have the potential to set in motion something that is far bigger and greater than yourself, and little will stop your adversaries as they attempt to keep that from happening. You will be criticized, rejected, bullied, and hated for doing what lesser minds think you cannot do.

"Twelve, twenty two, nineteen eighty-one,
Momma gave birth to another son.
But little did I know that growing up in the hood
Wouldn't be that good, 'cause, well, it was hell.
Where I dwell, in my home,
Didn't have no pops 'cause he gone.
And my momma, she was always working,
While me and my brother, we was always hurting.
And this was at the age of eight
And I'm thinking to myself, could this be my fate?
Thinking about my family with hate
And crying every night,
Hoping that someone would come and hold me tight
And tell me everything's okay.
But it wasn't that way.

It was just the opposite, asking God,
Why it had to be me and why couldn't I
Just have a happy family,
Without hearing my momma cry and my
daddy lie.
But that's when I made a declaration
That I would be someone in this nation.

"I wrote those words when I was fifteen years old. They were for a song I entitled, 'No Longer Locked Up.' You have to understand that I felt locked up when I was younger, both by my home situation and by my own insecurities. Regardless of what else was happening in my life, the truth was that opposition was already putting up bars to keep the greatness within me imprisoned. I knew that somehow I had to break free. I had no choice.

"Almost as soon as I was delivered from my mother's womb, I came face-to-face with resistance. I remember going to a furniture store as a boy with my mother. We were refused service there because my mother spoke limited English and, well, I didn't exactly look like a million bucks. Maybe it was the faded red Generra sweater, faded jeans, and worn-out shoes that gave away our family's income level, but somehow they knew. Regardless, I remember seeing the look on my mom's face and knowing right then that life was not easy.

"Even if they weren't directly aimed at me, whatever struggles my parents faced had an impact on my life as well. They were difficult to endure as a child, and they are difficult to revisit now. But—good or bad, right or wrong—they helped shape me into the man I have become today."

- A.C. Cristales

Everything that happens in our lives serves a purpose, even the arrival of adversity. Never question if opposition will come; its appearance is a certainty. It is a precursor to greatness, and we believe that greatness dwells within us all. What you must learn is how to make opposition work for you instead of allowing it to work you over. Harness it like the wind, and it will power your sails across the ocean of your dreams. Use it. Let it stoke the fire inside you until it burns brighter than the sun.

Up to this point, we have only mentioned opposition as being something brought against us by the people and circumstances that surround us. It would be a great disservice to you, however, if we failed to mention the most powerful enemy we can face. The reason this enemy is so formidable is because, unlike negative people and situations, it is one we can never truly escape. Why not?

Because this enemy is ourselves.

You see our greatest battle is not against flesh and blood, but rather against our own thoughts, our own insccurities, and our own disbelief. *We* are our own worst enemies when it comes to reaching our goals; we bring forth greater opposition than anyone or anything else ever could.

"For some time, I have wanted to make a living as a motivational speaker, author, and leadership consultant. It has not been easy. I have yet to be invited to a major conference. I have yet to sell a book or to address a grand audience. I press on despite these things, but my perseverance does not come easy. I face opposition just like anyone, and the opposition that does the most damage is that which I bring against myself.

"I limit what I can do by telling myself things can't be done; I wonder whether what I write has any substance or if what I am saying has any impact on those I speak to; I doubt my speaking abilities and question if anyone will ever invite me to speak to a gathering of thousands. I battle myself daily in these and many other areas, and sometimes this struggle takes its toll.

"It is a sad day when we—not the naysayers and not difficult circumstances—become the chief hindrance to living out the greatness within us. This is why it is so important to understand that the truest enemy we will face is really ourselves. Only by doing this can we defeat the internal antagonist before it defeats us."

- A.C. Cristales

You may wonder how we can ever hope to win such a struggle. Allow us to share an old Cherokee fable that we believe answers this question very well. It has come to be titled, *Two Wolves*.

An old Cherokee sat with his grandson, teaching him about life.

"A fight is going on inside me," he said to the boy. "It is a terrible fight, and it is between two wolves. One is evil—he is anger, envy, sorrow, regret, greed, arrogance, self-pity, guilt, resentment, inferiority, lies, false pride, superiority, and ego. The other is good—he is

71

joy, peace, love, hope, serenity, humility, kindness, benevolence, empathy, generosity, truth, compassion, and faith. This same fight is going on inside you—and inside every other person, too."

The grandson thought about it for a minute and then asked his grandfather, "Which wolf will win?"

The old Cherokee simply replied, "The one you feed."

Dreams do not realize themselves. We fulfill them through hard work, dedication, and faith. But our plans will not always turn out the way we want them to. There will be moments when they crash to the earth faster than falling stars and darken everything around us, especially our hopes. We must take care not to starve the first wolf and, by default, begin feeding the second when this happens.

"When I wrote *Cordero Keeper*, I believed great things were on the horizon. I was loving life because I was doing what I was passionate about, and I

had faith that things were really about to take off. I'd worked hard on that book, spending countless hours in the writing lab. Because I felt I had put in the necessary time, I also felt I deserved the abundance of life and assumed the universe was ready to serve it. But soon the rejection letters and emails began pouring in, each one a reality bite sinking its teeth into my heart and bringing greater self-doubt. I got angry; I became disillusioned. The evil wolf was being fed.

"I'd spend days at the bookstores and libraries reading the works of published authors and telling myself that I was better than them. As I began filling myself with a sense of false pride and ego, the evil wolf was feeding on my hate, becoming gluttonous while the other was starving. Who knows how much deeper into dejection I may have fallen had I not remembered something my mother used to always say to me: "*El que conoce hambre no gasta comida,"* the one who knows hunger doesn't waste food.

"Part of me was starving because I was denying it the nourishment it needed with my negativity. The good wolf had not died because it was seizing every morsel of the few positive feelings I was still desperately clinging to, but that would not have been true forever. I stopped being bitter and instead began being grateful for the opportunities to strengthen my character the rejection letters were allowing me. In that gratefulness, I started feeding the good wolf again and ultimately conquered the dissatisfaction and discontentment I felt."

- Axel Cristales

When it comes to measuring our success, the worst thing we can do is make comparisons between ourselves and others. Neither our worth nor our potential is determined by what someone else may have achieved. No, as we have said previously, both are determined by the amount of faith we place in ourselves and the steadfastness with which we pursue our dreams. If you want an accurate measure of success, measure it in terms of what you have endured, what you have survived in order to be where you are today. Never look at others and attempt to determine your value as a person.

"I remember being at a school assembly as a sixth-grader and having someone come to speak to us for career day. I don't remember who the gentleman was or what he did, but I do remember my response when he asked, 'What do you want to be when you grow up?'

"Most twelve-year-olds give generic answers like teacher, doctor, or football player when responding to that question. My response, however, was very specific. I said, 'I want to be a cardiovascular surgeon.' I don't even think I really knew what cardiovascular

meant, but I knew the career was one that would allow me to help people with heart issues. The fact that it also paid well didn't hurt.

"I can recall hearing my classmates snicker. I am sure even some teachers thought that dream was too far out of reach for a Hispanic kid like me, one who didn't always do the right thing. Regardless, their thoughts and opinions were not going to sway me from my following my dream. What did dissuade me was my great distaste for science, but that is another matter entirely.

"I may not have become a cardiovascular surgeon, but at least I can say that I am still helping people with heart issues, even if it is in a different way than I originally intended."

- A.C. Cristales

Life is hard, and it should be, especially for those who dream big. Nothing that is worth having, nothing that has true value, ever comes easily. Without struggle, without opposition, we will never acquire the endurance we need to survive in this world. A butterfly that is given assistance emerging from its cocoon, or a bird from its egg, will die soon thereafter. Because it was denied the opportunity to develop the strength necessary to survive in the world beyond, neither will ever soar to the heights they were intended. The same holds true for us.

We have shared about seeing our mother suffer physical abuse and about being abandoned by our father. These things, and many others he did as well, were far from easy to live through. But we chose at an early age to let them spark a fire in us to be bigger and better than any situation we could face. We were not trying then simply to make it out of the hood or to get by with decent paying jobs any more than today we are trying simply to buy nice houses and nice cars. We decided a long time ago that it would not be enough for us to just be two boys our mother would be proud of, but rather two grown men who could impact the world with our story. That is our dream—to make an impact on our generation, one that will not fade but will continue to resonate for those which follow.

It is up to you to discover your own dream. Even more importantly, once you do, it is up to you to ensure it comes true as well.

The bigger our dreams, the greater the number of adversaries we will face as we seek to make them realities. Like a pastor we heard once said, "The higher the levels, the greater the devils." But, no matter how many voices opposition may speak with or how many faces it may wear, the truth of the matter is that we can stand against them if we resolve to do so. They may weaken us at times, and occasionally we may feel inclined to surrender. But a successful person will endure at all costs. He or she will turn the table on opposition and makes something positive out of what was meant to be negative. You must always remember that neither your successes nor your failures truly mean anything to your detractors. They are inconsequential to their lives, merely topics of gossip at best. Stand against them. Let them be inconsequential to you as well.

No two people are the same. We are all given different gifts and talents, and we are all provided with different opportunities to use them. What we all share, however, is the presence of a unique and special treasure within us, one that only we can discover for ourselves. It is this treasure that the adversaries we face will attempt to steal from us. We must not allow them to do so.

You were meant to be different, and you were meant to use the talents and gifts you have been blessed with to do something amazing. Once you discover what that something may be, you must stand confidently in your purpose, even if that means you stand alone at times. Look over the course of your life and consider all you have already been through to get to where you are. Never underestimate the process that has shaped you and made you the person you have become.

In the past, perhaps you have allowed what others have thought or said about you to shape your future. Perhaps there have been times that your own thoughts and voice joined in the chorus speaking against you. But the fact that you are reading these words proves that you have endured and are still looking to the future, that you are still anticipating the myriad possibilities that await you. You have already overcome a great deal even to make it to this point in your life. You can and will overcome still more. That is what you were born to do.

There will always be naysayers around you. There will always be voices speaking negativity. But, just as kites rise highest when straining against the wind, so can you rise to your greatest heights when the forces of opposition come against you if only you will resist them. We can succeed in this endeavor by seeking reassurance in the face of discouragement and adversity, especially when the face it wears is our own.

What we hope to achieve through this book will not be easily accomplished, not due to a lack of desire or effort, but because it is always easier to destroy than it is to build. And that is what we hope our words will do—build you up, provide you with strength and confidence, assist you in discovering and pursuing your dreams. We urge you to surround yourselves with other men and women who will do the same. Be selective in your relationships. Do not assume that every friendly voice will always lift you up and do not assume that you can learn nothing from the voices of those more critical. Constructive criticism should always be welcomed as it is intended to help us identify areas in need of improvement as well as provide instruction on how to do so. Destructive criticism can become malignant if you let linger inside you. Heed constructive advice and disregard the rest.

You must hold on to this point; it is the key to understanding the fundamental truth of this course—the higher you set your sights, the farther your reach exceeds your grasp, the more opposition you will encounter. If you know this and still strive to move forward, you have already won a major battle, the first of many you will need to win in your pursuit of a greater life.

We close this course with some quotes that focus on opposition. May they inspire you just as they have inspired us.

"Obstacles are like wild animals. They are cowards but they will bluff you if they can. If they see you are afraid of them . . . they are liable to spring upon you; but if you look them squarely in the eye, they will slink out of sight."

- Orison Swett Marden

"You can measure a man by the opposition it takes to discourage him."

- Robert C. Savage

"Don't be distracted by criticism. Remember— the only taste of success some people have is when they take a bite out of you."

- Zig Ziglar

Opposition 101
Questions for Reflection

1. In the previous course, we discussed the fact that challenges are inevitable whenever we are climbing to reach a mountaintop. In this course, we discussed opposition, which is similar in that it is also inevitable, but is often a more direct and concerted attempt made either by others or even our own doubts, fears, and insecurities to derail us from our purposes. List some forms of opposition that you have faced to this point in your life. Identify if they came from internal or external sources and if they were successful in hindering you from reaching your goal.

2. Recall a time when someone told you that you were incapable of doing something you wanted to do. What feelings did you experience and how did they affect you? Did you allow this person to sway you from your purpose? If so, how and why? If not, why not and is this something you can keep in mind if it happens again in the future?

3. Create an action plan that you will use when someone tells you that you are unable to do something. How will you battle negative feelings that may arise? What affirmations will you give yourself in order to deal with the situation in a positive manner? What actions will you take, and which might you need to avoid, in order to keep moving forward?

4. The greatest enemy we can face is ourselves—the inner voices that speak negatively and make us question who we really are and what we are really capable of. How loudly does this enemy speak in your life? How much power do you allow it to have? What changes do you need to make in order to conquer it?

5. What stood out the most for you in this course and how will you apply that knowledge now?

Perseverance 101

Course Description

When challenges rise against you, when opposition presses in on all sides, it is natural to want to give up. Except for the presence of lingering disappointment, surrender is the easier road to follow. But true success never comes without resolve. When the going gets tough, some will let go rather than get going, but only those who are steadfast will move forward in life and achieve their dreams.

You have no doubt met with failure several times to this point your life, but you have almost certainly enjoyed success as well. The latter probably did not come easily, but rather at a cost. Will you cast your dreams aside in the face of adversity, allowing them to die without ever knowing how close you were to seeing them fulfilled, or will you hold on despite the discomfort and emerge victorious?

As aspiring speakers and writers, we try to learn what makes the "great ones"—orators and authors of world renown—great. We study their speaking and writing styles, their word choices and use of language, their presentation skills and means of grabbing and maintaining the attention of their audiences. More than anything else, however, we study their lives, specifically the obstacles and trials these men and women had to overcome on their paths to success. What we glean from our examinations we integrate into our own lives because, if there is one common thread of human character that links the past, present, and future, it is our ability to persevere.

As evidence of this, consider the example of a poor, single mother who once lived on welfare. Divorced and jobless, she had been diagnosed with depression and had even contemplated suicide. Then, while taking a train trip one day, she had an idea for a novel. She worked on her book in local cafes while her baby took naps in the stroller. Once her manuscript was finished, she submitted it for publication; it was rejected countless of times before a publishing house finally accepted it. This woman's birth name was Joanne Murray, but today people the world over know her as JK Rowling, author of the *Harry Potter* series.

In a commencement speech at Harvard, Rowling mentioned something about failure that we believe is very relevant to this course. She said, "Rock bottom became the solid foundation on which I rebuilt my life." She did not allow her difficulties to keep her mired in poverty, but rather endured them and, as a result, became the world's first female billionaire author. She is literally living the "rags to riches" fairy tale, all because she chose to persevere rather than surrender.

Struggles in life are unavoidable. As surely as the sun will rise, they will come. Some may batter us so badly that we will want to give up on everything we have planned, but that does not mean we must allow them to steal our hope. We can instead choose to see our trials simply as steps we must take along the path to greatness. This will not take our struggles away, but it can make them easier to bear and bring us a measure of peace. In that peace, we can find the strength to endure.

"I grew up idolizing Michael Jordan. As a thirteen-year-old kid whose dad had just walked out on him, I wanted to grab onto some sort of male role-model even if I had to reach through a thirteen-inch television screen to do it. I remember how I would check the television guide

hoping that a Bulls game would be showing that night. Back then I didn't know what greatness meant, but I had a sense I was watching it when I saw Air Jordan drive the lane, pull up over two opposing players, and hit the game winning shot.

"I remember reading a story about his days in high school, about how he'd been cut from his varsity sophomore basketball team. He went home, locked himself in his room, and cried. But despite his dejection, he kept working and working because, like the great ones do, he realized that not giving into defeat is the greatest victory a man can have. His quote, 'I've failed over and over in my life. That's why I succeed.' is one that has stayed with me since those days when I also would lock myself in my room and cry."

- Axel Cristales

According to the U.S. Census Bureau, twenty-four million children in America live in homes where the biological father is absent. One out of three children, thirty-three percent of our young men and women, are searching for an identity only a father can help them find. This was our dilemma growing up, both of us trying to discover who in the world we were.

Even though we earnestly believe that our mother did a tremendous job raising us, there were certain things she just could not teach us. There was a void in our lives that only our father's presence could have filled. His absence made us want to quit, not just in the classroom or in athletics, but in life as well.

"Several times in life I have felt like I wanted to quit. Many of them are associated with my father.

I remember being a teenager, waiting at the corner of Ridgewood and Dairy for my father to come see me. He was supposed to arrive at 6:00 p.m., but even when my watch displayed six o'clock, he wasn't there.

"Six fifteen. Not there.

"Six thirty. Not there

"I felt a great deal of sadness and disappointment over the fact that my dad didn't show up when he said he would, and I have often wondered why he chose not to come as he promised. As a teenager, I just figured he did not love me and that there were other things or people more important to him. Believe me when I say that is not a healthy way to grow up.

"What teenager gains happiness wondering why his father doesn't love him . . . or even if his father loves him at all?"

- A.C. Cristales

Our father's absence was just one of many difficult circumstances my brother and I encountered as children. Even when he was present, he was usually either drunk or high, and he was often violent as well.

Seeing our father abuse himself through his addiction to alcohol and drugs, then physically mistreat our mother unquestionably had an adverse effect on our lives. Indirectly, we were also being abused. We repeatedly wondered what the purpose of life was or if it was even worth living. It was difficult to maintain hope when pain clung to us like a dirty scent. We wanted to know what we had done to deserve a life like that. We each also wanted an answer to the even more pressing question, "Why am I here?" In writing this book, today we believe that we know the answer.

Perhaps you have asked yourself a similar question. Perhaps you are asking yourself that very thing right now. If so, let us give you a word of encouragement. *Everyone* has a purpose in this life, including you. It is the reason you were placed on earth, the reason you were granted the talents and gifts you possess. It may take years for you to find out exactly what you are meant to do, but that does not matter. Your purpose will be revealed to you at exactly the right time for you to take action. Knowing this, knowing that you have a *why* in life, can help you find the *will* in it when things do not seem to be going your way.

"I recently spoke to a group of high school seniors, and one question that came up was, 'Is college hard?' My response was an honest in that I said yes, but then I explained that life itself is also hard and that the key to succeeding in one is the same as succeeding in the other. We do not have to always be the strongest, the smartest, or the most talented, but we do have to be willing to endure hardship with a strong will and sense of purpose.

"I asked these students if they knew who Michael Jordan was. Some of them pointed to the logo on their sneakers. I then asked if they knew who Abraham Lincoln was. Some of them nodded to the poster of the U.S. Presidents hanging on the wall. When I followed this question with another asking how many knew who JK Rowling was, one of the students took one of the Harry Potter books out of her backpack and showed it to me 'For every Jordan, Lincoln, and

Rowling,' I told them, 'there are thousands of people we have never heard of, people who could have been just as great if only they hadn't given up." Then I asked them something that I sincerely hope remains with them still, 'How will your name be remembered?'

"Think about that the next time you're at a point where you feel ready to give up."

- Axel Cristales

Persistence is a quality many people admire, but few actually possess. It is also a trait that must be cultivated over time. The first step in this process is recognizing that you do, in fact, have a purpose in life. If there is any doubt of this in your mind, it will rob you of your ability to endure when difficulties arise.

"One of the greatest failures in my life came about while I was writing my first novel, *Cordero Keeper*. For six months I worked diligently writing what I believed in my heart was going to be a great book. I was on fire. I remember

spending ten-hour days in the basement of the library putting my heart on paper. Then something happened to me, to that certainty of purpose that burned inside of me. I allowed the storms of criticism and rejection to shipwreck my dream. Who knows what could have happened if I had persisted. I failed only because I stopped trying."

- Axel Cristales

Do not live a life filled with regret wondering what could have been. If you aspire to greatness, you must battle through whatever difficulties life brings your way. You will never achieve anything significant or worthy of celebration if you flee from adversity rather than take a stand against it. Remember, it is the acorn that holds its ground today that grows into the mighty oak of tomorrow.

There is a saying in Spanish, "*Donde hubo fuego quedan cenizas.*" One translation for this expression is, "Old flames die hard." Although it is often used to describe old romantic relationships, we believe it is also relevant here because if you have enough passion for your goals and dreams, you will allow nothing and no one to keep you from achieving them.

I have always been amazed by how many people compromise their talents and gifts in order to settle for any measure of success within their reach. Initially they may find comfort in this and perhaps even a sense of security. After enough time passes, however, they invariably find disappointment as well. We have been there.

We used to live by the phrase, "The sky's the limit." Then we realized that it was not the sky limiting us at all, but rather ourselves. We wanted the easy way out, we wanted shortcuts . . . and we found them. All we did by pursuing these things, however, was hinder our own potential. Having traveled both, we can honestly say that the path of greatest resistance has always served us far better in our journey along the road to success than its lesser counterpart. We believe the same holds true for everyone.

We challenge you now to discover this for yourself. Determine your purpose and allow it to become the acorn from which the oak of your future will grow. Make no mistake, you will be tried along your path. Problems will arise to test your perseverance time and time again. In themselves they will not negate your potential for greatness, though they may perhaps bring about a delay in seeing it recognized. No, you will fail these tests only if you surrender. Steel yourself today for the challenges and opposition that will arise tomorrow, then push through them when they do. Succeed where others fail by resolving to do so at this moment.

Remember, purpose precedes perseverance, and perseverance supersedes problems.

There are three things we would like you to remember as you prepare yourself to move forward:

1. At times, people fail to persevere because, at some point, they allow doubt and disbelief to rob them of their purpose.

    Purpose without self-belief is like a car without an engine—no matter how many times you attempt to get started and set out, you will never go anywhere. Delays and even failures are less a reflection on us than they are on the unpredictable nature of life.

Do not allow interruptions or setbacks to cause you to stop believing either in yourself or in your purpose.

2. At times, people fail to persevere because, gifted though they may be, they allow their difficulties to steal their focus.

   Talent will only take us so far. Without a plan, without a map to direct our course, reaching a destination will be incredibly difficult, if not impossible. As much as we are able, we should outline the course we will follow to reach our goals, then adhere to it. Do not allow the trials that will inevitably arise to distract you. Plan your course, including the alternate paths you can take when troubles come, and put your plan into action.

3. At times, people fail to persevere because they become so impatient they simply give up on their dreams.

   We do not receive things in life simply because we demand them. We must work for them; what we earn is a return on what we have endured. Many people give up on the goals they are working toward because they cannot reach them at the exact moment they would like to. The truth is, there are times when we *need* to experience delays in order to ensure that we are mature enough to handle blessings when they do arrive. Consider not only what you want to receive out of life, but also how determined you are to earn it, how long you are willing to work and wait to see your dreams fulfilled.

Fulfilling your purpose will take conviction, an unshakeable faith both in yourself and in what you are doing, what you are working toward. It will require a certainty of focus that no measure of adversity will sway. It may take longer than you want or are willing to wait, perhaps years or even an entire lifetime. But, if it means anything to you at all, you will remain determined enough to see it through.

"Recently, I spoke to a group of high school students about motivation. These

students had been part of a program which was designed to motivate them to make better decisions. The program did a phenomenal job of getting the kids excited. While they were engaged, I asked them what they were going to do when that motivation faded away. I wanted them to consider what they would do when yesterday's motivations were confronted by today's tribulations?

"I challenged them to ensure that they put some P.E.P. in their step—persistence, endurance, purpose. Many of us love attending sporting events because the music, the chants, the drama, and the atmosphere all come together to create an unforgettable experience. We love motivational rallies and inspirational stories because they have the ability to make us feel like we are Superman or Wonder Woman and that we can take on anything in the world.

"I am not knocking these things. They stir emotions deep inside of us. They get us excited, pump us up, charge our spirits. I am a huge motivator myself, so I love the enthusiasm they generate. Still, I know that excitement eventually fades away. After the celebration, nothing remains of these things except memories.

"Pursuing our dreams cannot be solely about motivation. If it is, when challenging circumstances arise and steal that motivation away, we will be left with nothing. We must also be determined, so much so that no one and nothing can long hinder us. Our character must be built upon these traits because once they are engrained in us, they will not fade away.

"What characteristics define you? What is your foundation built upon? What is going to keep you from not giving up?"

- A.C. Cristales

When things get challenging, we are often told to look at the glass being half full rather than half empty. After experiencing enough setbacks, however, it is easy to not only see the glass as being half empty, but also full of cracks. If we are not careful, we may stop reaching for it altogether.

You must not allow this to happen in your own life. As certainly as opportunities are to present themselves, just as certainly will challenges come and opposition arise threatening to hinder you from achieving your dreams. Not only must you stand against them, but also against the temptation to give up when life does not unfold as you hope or expect. Despite all odds, you must persist, for the "great ones" are meant to persevere.

When you get knocked down, get up and keep fighting. When you are told no, tell yourself yes and find another way. Do not sabotage your dreams because of momentary setbacks. Do not make temporary failure permanent defeat. Without a willingness to stand amidst the storms of life we cannot know true achievement in any form.

As we bring this lesson to a close, we would like to remind you to always walk with persistent, enduring, and purposeful steps. Because what you do daily determines what you receive daily, we would also like to encourage you to give yourself this P.E.P. talk everyday:

"I will persist on the unknown road understanding that every step not taken is a step backwards in fulfilling my purpose. I will endure the turbulent times knowing that my success hinges not on if I fall in the pit, but rather on if I fall in the pit and remain there. I will be purposeful in my pursuit and remain steadfast on my road toward success even when I do not see what I know in my heart has been promised to me."

Once again we would like to leave you with some quotes that we have found inspirational. We sincerely hope that they will inspire greater perseverance within you.

"I am here for a purpose and that purpose is to grow into a mountain, not to shrink to a grain

of sand. Henceforth, I will apply all my efforts to become the highest mountain of all, and I will strain my potential until it cries for mercy."

- Og Mandino

"Every defeat, every heartbreak, every loss, contains its own seed, its own lesson on how to improve your performance the next time."

- Og Mandino

"He who has a why to live can bear almost any how."

- Friedrich Nietzsche

Perseverance 101
Questions for Reflection

1. No one is immune to failure. It is simply a part of our journey along the path to success. What are your personal feelings toward failure? Do you agree that failure should never be allowed to overtake you or crush your inner spirit? What could the consequences of allowing this be?

2. We believe that everyone on earth has a purpose in life. What do you believe your purpose is and what steps can you take both now and in the future to see it fulfilled? If you are still unsure of what your purpose is, identify something that you feel passionately about and explain how you can create a living out of it.

3. What do you foresee being potential hindrances to achieving the goals you have set for yourself? How will you stay encouraged when those hindrances arise and bring your forward momentum to a stop?

4. In this course we warn you about falling victim to three potential dangers: self-doubt, lack of focus, and impatience. Which of these three do you feel poses the greatest threat to you? What will you do to avoid allowing it to derail you from your purpose?

5. We would like to ask you the same question A.C. asked his students. What will you do when yesterday's motivations are confronted by today's tribulations? What will you do to maintain your determination to press on?

Habits 101

Course Description

Regardless of whether they are harmful or healthy, our behaviors eventually become habits if engaged in long enough. Behaviors that suppress our potential are the allies of failure, while those that are empowering aid us in achieving our goals. Just as we are products of our environments, so are our failures and successes products of our habits. How our lives unfold in the future is dependent on the habits we form today.

Do you desire success? Do you aspire for greatness? The degree to which you will achieve these things, or if you will achieve them at all, is dependent upon the habits you display even at this moment. Will you allow bad habits to hinder you, both now and in the future, or will you resolve to cast them aside and instead develop habits that will advance your goals and dreams?

You and I, along with every other person in the world, have two things in common. First, for each of us, the clock is ticking and the hour of our last breath is drawing nearer. Secondly, our characters are being shaped every single day by the habits we engage in.

Developing bad habits is an easy trap to fall into because they are often quick and easy to perform and provide short-term relief when things do not go our way. At times they may appear harmless, but ultimately they do nothing more than distract us from our true purposes. We will never reach our full potential if these are the only habits we form in our lives. To make matters worse, once they are adopted, they are very difficult to break without proper guidance and assistance.

A wealthy man requested the aid of an old scholar to assist in weaning his son away from his bad habits.

One day, the scholar took the youth for a stroll through a garden. Stopping suddenly he asked the boy to pull out a tiny plant growing there. The youth held the plant between his thumb and forefinger and pulled it out. The old man then asked him to pull out a slightly bigger plant. The youth pulled hard and the plant came out, roots and all.

"Now pull out that one," said the old man pointing to a bush. The boy had to use all his strength to pull it out.

"Now take this one out as well," said the old man, indicating a guava tree standing nearby. The youth grasped the trunk and tried to pull it out. But it would not budge.

"I – It's impossible," said the boy, panting with the effort.

"So it is with bad habits," said the sage. "When they are young it is easy to pull them out but when they take hold they cannot be uprooted."

The session with the old man changed the boy's life.

Fortunately, good habits are as easily formed as their negative counterparts. Quite often they fail to receive the same degree of attention, but they absolutely must be recognized when they are displayed. Much more than that, their development must be encouraged. Create good habits and we will create victories as well . . . perhaps only small ones at first, but victories nonetheless. Each small victory we experience will increase our momentum as we advance closer to our goals.

Take a moment to review your life. If you look closely enough, what you will see repeated over and over again is that one action was directly responsible for bringing about a series of others. These chain reactions, whether you were aware of it or not, shifted the patterns of your life and shaped the habits you later developed. We are certain that many of these habits have been good, but you would not be human if you had not allowed some bad habits to develop as well. The important factors to consider are which you possess in greater number and how much influence they exert upon your life today.

Habits are powerful forces that change our sense of who we are and what we believe. If we want to ensure that our futures are the best they can possibly be, we must cultivate good habits on a daily basis, and we must start doing this as early in our lives as possible.

"Honk! Honk! Honk!

"My mom had no shame honking her horn when picking me up after school. In fact, she was so good at it, I told her to pick me up at the corner so she wouldn't have the opportunity to show off her honking skills to my friends waiting there on the front porch.

"Growing up, I was afraid of my mother. She is only five feet tall, so this wasn't because she was an imposing figure. My mom just had something about her that made me fear her. Maybe it was getting disciplined with a *chancla* (flip flop) or better yet, a *mata-mosca* (fly swatter).

All kidding aside, the reason I was afraid of my mom was because of her presence and what she expected, which was simply that I respect her. She expected me to hold my tongue and not talk back to her, even though there were many times that I did. She expected me to stay out of trouble at school, although there were many times that I did not. She

111

expected me to do something with my life rather than sit on my butt while she busted hers for my brother and I.

"In short, my mother expected me to learn, and learn I did . . . even if it meant getting into her car and heading out to work instead of playing football with my friends. She was determined to teach me that if I worked hard, I would never lack anything I needed. Her method of instruction was not by lecture. No, her method of instruction was to use the best learning strategy possible—engagement.

"Yes, when she would honk her horn, I would run to the car, enter it, buckle my seat belt, and enjoy the Latin music my mom was listening to. But I also knew it was time for me to learn."

- A.C. Cristales

Growing up we had two educations, one provided by our teachers and the other by our mother. During the day, we received the standard English, math, science, and computer skills lessons. In the evenings and on the weekends, we received "real world" instruction, namely how to earn our keep by cleaning daycare centers, churches, and small business offices. Those were simply the cards we had been dealt. Folding them would have meant starving, so that was the way it had to be. My father was not going to come back and save us. Whatever salvation was to come had to come first from within. We had to develop good work habits very early just to survive.

"Despite the pain caused by the hardships of my family, I gained a great deal as an eight-year-old janitor. One lesson in particular that I learned was that hard work paid off. I didn't know it at the time and my mom didn't plan it, but it was by working after school and on the weekends that I developed one of the habits that carried me through my teenage and college years and still serves me now in my early thirties—the habit of

waking up every morning knowing that the world was not going to hand me what I wanted simply because I wanted it.

"No, it was through helping my mother—at times by choice and at times more reluctantly because I would have rather been playing Mortal Kombat with my boys—that I learned how to earn what I wanted with hard work. From that point on, whatever I set out to do, I did it working hard.

"At eighteen, I was promoted to Lead Customer Service Representative after being with a company for only six months. At twenty-one, I was teaching my first bilingual class during the day while still finishing my Bachelor's degree at night. At twenty-three, I received my Master's degree and a few months later, at twenty four, I was appointed assistant principal in the second largest school district in Dallas

County. All of these things I achieved because I worked hard to do so."

- A.C. Cristales

Was growing up this way always easy? No, of course not. In fact, as we have shared several times throughout these courses, growing up as we did was incredibly challenging. We could have chosen a different path. Rather than digging in our heels and pushing forward toward success, we could have chosen quicker and easier paths to earn the money we needed to survive, illegal paths that would have accomplished little else than reduce us to statistics. But we did not. Despite what our upbringing was, despite what the numbers predicted we would become, we always believed there was greatness inside us. Somehow we knew that one day we would graduate college and hold degrees, that we would have a positive influence on the lives of other people, that somehow our hell would become a blueprint for others so that they could enjoy a little heaven on earth. The belief that greatness dwelt within us is what shifted our thinking as we were growing older.

Everything begins with belief, even change.

Was life unfair? It certainly seemed that way growing up. As we grew older, however, we also grew wiser. We stopped putting our focus on our lack of a father-figure and instead focused on how blessed we were to have a mother who wore two hats. Questions such as, "Why did our dad leave us?" and "Why were we forced to start working at such an early age?" began to be less and less important. We still cried, but the belief that we were capable of becoming so much more than we then were, knowing there were people who would help us make that belief a reality, helped us realize that we were living just a small part of a much greater story.

"As my thoughts and perspective changed so did the words that I let flow from my heart.

"I used to tell my mother that I hated her because I resented her for not doing enough to hold onto my father. Those words instead became 'I love you.' I once damned myself and others with harsh words of condemnation, but learned instead to say, 'Thank you, God.' when I

struggled against adversity. Once I learned to stop speaking death into my life, I allowed words of affirmation to begin flowing out of me. I permitted myself to believe that my brother and I were going to contribute something of value to this world, and I confirmed that with my words. 'We,' I would tell him, 'are destined for greatness.'

"But I didn't stop there. I put those words to work. I believe strongly in my faith. One of the many things it has taught me is that belief without action is dead. God will always meet us halfway if we only take that first step. So I lived out my teenage years doing all forms of labor—scrubbing toilets, vacuuming rooms in childcare centers, serving as a lifeguard, stacking wood, sorting toys and CDs at a retail store, working collections, handling packages at FedEx—all in the name of paying for college. My mom did what she could to help me out, but primarily I did it on my own. The greatest sense of accomplishment I had as a result, other than being the first grandchild out of over thirty on my dad's side of the family to graduate with a college degree, was that I did so without incurring debt.

"These actions influenced my habits later in life. While working toward my Bachelor's degree, I learned to save money, to value my family, to be proactive and responsible, to smile even through the rain and pain. I learned to put first things first, to visualize good things on a daily basis, and to pray.

"Yes, my habits showed me what things to value, what things were worth my time. These values began shaping my destiny, even then. They still are."

- Axel Cristales

When we think about our most fulfilling days, they are not days we spent lounging around doing nothing. They have been those when it felt as though the deck was stacked against us, when we had so much work to do we thought we would never see the end, yet still persevered no matter what came our way . . . just as we are doing now while writing this book.

Understand that the praise and accolades we communicate to you are not shared to impress you. We simply want to give you an accurate understanding of everything we have endured and the affirmations we have employed in the hopes that you, too, can put them to use and move past your present struggles to achieve as we have. We are what we continually do; we cease to be that which we cease to do. Our habits are a testament to our character.

This same concept holds true for you.

We can proudly say that everything we have achieved we have earned because of the habits we have displayed throughout our lives. No free rides were given to us. No one took pity on us or sought to do the work for us when they saw two young boys struggling to carry bags of trash out to the dumpsters in dark alleys. No one entered our graduate class and singled us out saying, "I am going to promote you both to be leaders in my school." It was our habits that made it possible for us to succeed in our personal and professional lives, and our habits were formed through our daily routines.

If you want an accurate predictor of what your future will hold, look closely at what your routines are today. Your success, or lack thereof, will be almost wholly dependent upon them.

Self-management expert Brian Tracy says, "Successful people are simply those with successful habits." A renowned speaker who has shared his insights in more than eighty countries on six continents, Tracy's success was not something he was born with or inherited. Brian Tracy grew up in a poor family, dropped out of school, and lived in boarding homes. When he turned twenty-one he found a job on a Norwegian freighter that provided him the opportunity to travel around the world. After two years, he tired of that and accepted a job earning commission on sales. During that time Tracy began to wonder what made some people more successful than others. He began reading books on the subject, books on selling techniques and on what elevated the best salespeople to such a position. He then emulated what they did. Six months later, he was the top salesman in his company. He painstakingly studied the habits of successful people then adopted them in his life as well.

So many times we think we know what it takes to be successful but do nothing with that knowledge. Those who achieve, however, are the people who have developed and maintained habits conducive to that end. Malcolm Gladwell, author of the book *Outliers*, wrote the following after studying the most successful men and women in a number of different professions, "It takes roughly 10,000 hours of practice to achieve mastery in any field." Once again the same truth is expressed—for better or for worse, those things we do on a consistent basis directly affect the course of our lives. Who we are today and who we will be in the future are in large part determined by our habits.

Who are you right this moment? Who do you wish to be tomorrow?

As we draw this course to a close, we would ask you to consider those questions carefully. If you are not satisfied with your answers, with your evaluation of your position either at present or what you foresee it being in the future, we would like to remind you that there is still hope, still time to change your beliefs, your habits, and the course of your life.

If you sincerely desire change . . .

Make the decision today—right this very moment—to manage your thinking. Cast aside all negative thoughts. The moment something negative enters your mind, dismiss it and replace it with something positive. If your past affects your present, think about your future and what you must do to change it. As James Allen wrote, "A man is literally what he thinks, his character being the complete sum of all his thoughts." Therefore resolve to watch your thoughts because what you think will be what you speak.

Make the decision today—right this very moment—to speak positively about yourself and others. The power of life and death dwells in your words. They can be either fruit or poison for your soul and the souls of others. With them you will either build up or tear down. Do not tell yourself you cannot do something. Tell yourself not only that you *can*, but also that you *will*. Do not say your situation is hopeless. Say instead that is challenging and that it is only a matter of time before you overcome your challenges and move on. Watch your words for, as Rabbi Leon Da Modena says, "Words are the guides to actions. The mouth makes the first move." Therefore resolve to watch your words because what you say will become what you do.

Make the decision today—right this very moment—to act in a manner that will bring you closer to your goals. Do not waste a single day by doing nothing. Know that in order to succeed you must daily take steps toward your goals and dreams. Choose to take action today because, as Thomas Jefferson once said, "Do you want to know who you are? Don't ask. Act! Action will delineate and define you." Therefore resolve to watch your actions because they are vital to shaping your habits.

Make the decision today—right this very moment—to manage your routine and agenda. Choose to live intentionally, to develop new habits and, in turn, develop a new you. Do not fear stepping beyond your comfort zone. Understand that in order to receive something you have never had, you will have to do some things you have never done. Develop new habits and remember the words of a Frank Crane who said, "Habits are safer than rules; you don't have to watch them. And you don't have to keep them either. They keep you." Therefore resolve to watch your habits because people will identify you by them.

Make the decision today—right this very moment—to live a life of integrity. Choose to be fair and forgiving towards others. Understand that what you do, rather than what you say, is how people identify your character, and that character ultimately determines how you will be remembered. Theodore Roosevelt said it best, "Character, in the long run, is the decisive factor in the life of an individual and nations alike." Therefore, above all, resolve to watch your character because your future—your destiny— depends on it.

Cast aside those habits that are hindering your growth and replace them with behaviors that advance you in the pursuit of your dreams. Build a better and brighter future for yourself, and begin doing so today.

Habits 101
Questions for Reflection

1. Identify at least three of your good habits and explain how they have aided you in reaching your goals in the past. Identify at least three bad habits that you believe you have as well. Explain how they may have prevented you from being what you want to be and doing what you really want to do.

2. Sometimes, we feel we are doing certain things when, in reality, we are not. Ask a friend or family member to communicate with you some of the habits they see you consistently practice. How many of these were good habits and how many were bad?

3. We can form new habits by changing our beliefs and the way we view things. What are some beliefs you now realize you must have in order to form good habits?

4. Now that you have completed this course, we hope you understand the importance of establishing positive behaviors and routines. Create a daily

agenda for yourself, a routine you can honestly adhere to. Remember, this may not be easy to do at first, but do not waver. Follow through with it and you *will* see your positive habits drawing you closer to fulfilling your goals.

5. Write down the habits your friend or family member shared with you and reflect on their answers.

Family 101

Course Description

No man or woman is an island. Despite what we may think or tell ourselves at times, none of us can exist all alone. We need others in our lives; we need relationships with people we value and who value us in return. We must take care when determining which relationships to invest our time in and which we may need to avoid, however, as our emotional attachments can make this a difficult matter to settle.

It will require both wisdom and courage in order to decide which relationships you should strengthen and which you should sever. Are you willing to conduct an honest evaluation of your current associations, resolving to ensure that only those which are healthy remain? What if this means you must love from afar friends you have known your entire life or perhaps even members of your own family? Will you agree to distance yourself from those individuals who impede your growth and advancement toward your goals, or will you instead continue allowing them to hinder you?

Some people have a narrow interpretation of exactly who constitutes family, while others favor a much broader definition. As we have attempted to make clear in previous courses, we firmly believe that family is everything. What is more, we also consider it to be composed of individuals united by bonds of love, not simply by blood.

For the purpose of this course, we would like to ask you to view family as consisting of those individuals who see our imperfections, but still choose to accept us just as we are because they realize they are not perfect either; those individuals who do not tally all of our wrongs, but instead remind us of those things we do well because they believe in us even when we may not believe in ourselves; those individuals who love us unconditionally and are always at our side no matter what circumstances arise because they know we will be there for them as well.

The truth of the matter is, we are human turnstiles. People come into and out of our lives virtually every day, but only a select few remain with us for an extended period of time. It is vital that we have those few with us for as long as we can, however. As human beings, we can endure the lack of many things. But loneliness, the absence of connections with other people, can be extremely difficult to bear.

We were made for relationships. Our interactions with others teach us, shape us, guide us. We need other people in our lives because no matter how passionate we may be about our goals and aspirations, there will come points when our enthusiasm begins to dwindle, when we get tired, when we stop dreaming, stop hoping. There will be times when it will be absolutely necessary for us to have other people to push us, to encourage us, and to rekindle the fire inside of us. These individuals are the true soldiers we can count on through thick and thin, those who stand with us and join in our struggles so we do not have to fight alone.

Be they friends or family members, we must treasure these people with all of our hearts, for they are indispensable to us and to our well-being. They help us find peace in troubling times and bolster our faith when doubts and insecurities assail us. They refuse to criticize us, leaving judgment instead solely to the providence of the Creator. Though they may press us and push us to do our best, they never attempt to compete with us or outshine us because they recognize that there is room enough in the spotlight for us all. They love us truly and commit themselves to helping us along our paths even as they also walk their own, sharing their wisdom and receiving ours because they recognize that we are stronger together than we can ever be alone. Like the air, though they may at times be silent, still they are always present to sustain us.

By contrast, false friends or self-centered family members flee when times become challenging and return only when our troubles pass. Like the rain that falls and then moves on, they come into and out of our lives as they please. When they are present, they often speak negatively, criticizing us and exacerbating our fears because, consciously or otherwise, they are afraid that we will do and become what they could only dream of. Rather than feeling joy when they see us attaining great things, they feel envy and jealousy. They allow their own bruised egos and insecurities to get the better of them, and they attempt to foster the same poison in us. Individuals such as these can eventually decimate our spirits if we allow them to do so.

It is never easy to say goodbye to people who have been with us for long periods of time, but sometimes that is precisely what we must do. At some point, we all must take inventory of our lives and look carefully at the relationships we have fostered and are continuing to feed or, perhaps more appropriately, are allowing to feed on us. If we are not careful, if we refuse to check our unhealthy relationships, we are actually sacrificing our chances at fulfilling our greater purposes in life. Negative people, selfish people, hurtful people—they add no value to our lives. We can never advance in any manner through them or because of them. Perhaps that seems like a cruel thing to say, but sometimes truth is a painful pill to swallow. Negative relationships steal our energy and our focus from other, far healthier concerns. For this reason, we must guard our hearts against them. What we feed our hearts determines how we live. Out of them, the wellsprings of our lives flow. We must watch after and protect them because, once they are wounded or broken, life becomes much more difficult to bear.

We will never lose those who are true to us. Only those who were never truly invested in their relationships with us ever really disappear from our lives. If you want to know how to determine the difference between the two, ask yourself how much value they add to your life, how much you gain as a human being because of your association with them and how much you give in return. For those relationships of true worth, such things will be impossible to measure.

"There are three members of my family who have really made an impact on me. In his or her own unique way, each has exhibited the same love and loyalty at some period of my life, either good or bad. Because of them, I have learned that the truest bonds are formed in the throes of battle.

"First among them is my mother. Over the years she has softened, but when I was younger and we would go to the grocery store, she was the kind of woman who would beat me (in a loving way) even before I got out of the car. Every time this would happen, I would ask, 'Mom, why'd you hit me? I didn't do anything.' To this she would always reply, 'That's just in case you ask me for anything when we get inside the store.'

Even now, after I've given her two beautiful grandchildren, she gets onto me the same way she always did.

"But my mother is my mother, and I love her just as she is. She is the kind of woman who allows her actions to speak for her, a woman of few words but a great deal of work. Whenever I'm going through something, I can go to her. She won't say much, but she'll get in that kitchen and cook me up a four-course meal in no time. Once she puts it in front of me, in my heart it's greater than hearing the words, 'I love you.' No matter how I may fail, though she may challenge me, she never judges me. 'No person is worthy of throwing stones,' she has always said. Together we've endured a broken home, working two or three jobs in order to pay the bills, and going our separate ways when I got married. We still endure disappointments in life to this day. But throughout everything, we have loved and remained true to one another.

"My father is on the other side of the spectrum. For several years, we did not talk. He divorced my mother when my brother and I were young, and he was in and out of my life throughout my high school years. I preferred it to be this way most of the time because when he was in it, things were not good. He was sent to prison for three years for drug-related offenses, but despite that, he still remained loyal to me in his own way. I have learned that it just takes longer for some people to grow up, and I've seen that kind of change in my dad over the years.

"If my mom is one of few words, then my dad is one I sometimes wish would shut up. All joking aside, I don't mean that at all because he has so much to offer in terms of wisdom and love. I still remember when our relationship changed. One Monday morning I received a call from him. I had just accomplished my dream of publishing my own book, *Cordero Keeper*. I don't remember when or how he'd received a copy, but in his phone call to me, I can still hear the elation and pride in his voice as he told me how very talented I was. He told me that he had always believed in me and that he wanted me to write more books so he could show them off and give them to his friends. Even though my book was a 'worst-seller,' that phone call made me believe in myself and in my abilities. Because of this one event, my dad and I have now struck up a solid relationship. If I need advice or someone to listen to me when I want to unload about the valleys in life, I seek him out. This never would have been possible if my father hadn't been honest with me and loved me without judgment . . . or if I had failed to do the same for him.

"Last, but not least, there's my brother, my goodfella, my soldier. He is a perfect combination of both my mother and father. At times he speaks; at times he remains silent. Regardless of his words or actions, however, his love is always evident. We've cried together—then cried together some more—but mostly we've laughed, so much so that, by the end of the crying, we could ultimately say, 'We're going to be good.'

"He could probably offer you as much insight about having true friends and family as I can since I've lived my entire life loving and being loyal to him. We have shared a lot of great memories. The best memory I have of us 'going to war' together—besides the battle we find ourselves in right now writing this book—was the night I went buckwild on people who had hurt him. He was 14 years old; I was 18. We'd gone to church one Wednesday night as we normally did every week. In the midst of all that was happening around us, we lost ourselves to God. Church, we believed, could be a refuge, and it was. But we soon learned the meaning of the word, 'fake.'

"My brother and I have always been dreamers. At that age we thought this was a good thing, but we soon learned that sometimes having dreams causes people to hate you. I had always been sort of a rebellious figure, in a good way if that's possible. I always questioned things when I didn't think they were fair. I didn't do this because I wanted to be defiant, but rather because I never wanted to just follow the crowd or lack the courage to blaze new trails. This rubbed a lot of people the wrong way.

"My baby brother looked up to me. He saw me as a father-figure, so he took on my personality at an early age. When I left church that night with my girlfriend, my brother stayed back with one of our

cousins to hang out with some of our friends. Although I did not know this at the time, people were not kind to him afterwards. I assumed everything was cool until he got home and walked through the door crying. Immediately furious, I charged up to the church and went off on everyone I could find who had made my brother feel bad, everyone who had said hurtful things to him.

"I used to think that I lost a lot of friends that day, but as I go through life, I now realize you can't lose friends, at least not the true ones."

- Axel Cristales

In the book of Proverbs, Scripture says, "A brother is born for adversity." At first glance, it may seem like that verse means that two siblings will always fight or otherwise be at odds with one another. That is hardly what King Solomon had in mind when he recorded those words, however. What he actually meant was that a brother will be there for you through the hardest moments of your life. He will not abandon you, even in the face of things that cause you both to tremble. Instead, he will find the courage to get in the trenches and fight with you because if you die, part of him dies too.

My brother and I have been blessed to have each other through the most adverse moments in our lives. Other than our mother, we were all we had growing up. Fortunately, we were all we really needed anyway. We often talk about the times the three of us would go clean daycare centers together. We all had a task and, as much we may have hated it, we did what we had to do in order to help one another. It was during those times that we felt our love for one another being expressed more sincerely through the others' actions than ever could have been shared in words.

One of my mother's dreams for us has been that we succeed at whatever we set our minds to. Even more than that, however, she has always wanted us to remain together. We are glad to say that, to this point in our lives, we have made our mother's dream a reality. My brother and I are best friends. This does not mean that we are not rivals at times or that we do not say things that disappoint each other, but despite these things, our bond remains strong. Adversity reveals who your true family is, and we have proven that we are true to each other time and again.

"Axel's been my best friend for a long time. He has been there when I felt alone and defeated; he has served as a father-figure to me when I did not know what to do. He was the first one I spoke to when I discovered I was going to be a father. He has been there through my greatest joys, but even more importantly, he has been there through the lowest moments of life as well.

"For me, that is what family is about . . . knowing that when the storm comes, I'm going to have somebody to dance in the rain with. Sure life can and will be painful, but when you have a true brother, you know you have someone who was born to endure the adversity with you. I am blessed, and I'm proud to say that I have always been blessed. In

spite of the fact that I grew up without a father, my mother courageously took on the role of being both parents for me. I have had a brother who has stuck by me through thick and thin. As Dan Wilcox says, 'I don't care how poor a man is, if he has family, he's rich.'

"Maybe I didn't have the best clothes growing up or drive the most luxurious car in high school, but I was still the richest man in the world. Why?

"Because I had family."

- A.C. Cristales

We cannot survive without others who care for us; they are as real as it gets. They will always be the people in our lives who also want us to be a part of theirs, the people who accept us for who we are. They are the people who would do anything to see us smile and who will love us no matter what, even if it means sacrificing a little of who they are. We must learn to truly appreciate family, whether they are joined to us by bonds of blood or of love, because they stand with us through the ups and downs of this life without flinching and without hesitation. Hopefully they will all one day stand alongside us in heaven as well.

"'I didn't say that,' I sobbed as I pleaded my case, hoping Mr. Drummond would believe me.

"'You know you said that. Don't lie to me.'

"'I didn't. I promise. I said, "Forget you."'

"'Come on, Abiezer. Do you seriously think I am going to believe that?'

"Sure enough, Mr. Drummond did not believe that I said, 'Forget you.' He was right to disbelieve me, but as an eleven-year-old, I had no option but to be a trickster and try to manipulate my way out of being in trouble.

"I knew that the four letter 'f-word' directed at Mrs. Craig was going to place me in hot water even before it left my lips. There was no justification for saying that to her, even if she was interrupting me while I was trying to flirt with a beautiful girl—Angie Coleman. I knew better than to speak to an adult, or anyone else for that matter, in that way. My mother had taught me better than that, but at that moment I wasn't thinking about what my mom would say. In fact, I don't think I was thinking about anything except what I would say to Angie Coleman had she given me her phone number.

"Needless to say, my choice of words immediately caused an uproar in the classroom, not to mention with Mrs. Craig. As soon as I blurted those words out of my mouth, the entire class turned around like I had passed gas and released a collective, 'Ooohhh.' That was all Mrs. Craig needed to send me outside in the hallway so she could continue her lessons on adjectives and, of course, so she could write a referral for me to have a one-on-one appointment with the principal.

"They say everyone has a breaking point. Well, I believe that applies to teachers and administrators just as much as anyone else. I learned that firsthand sitting across from Mr. Drummond that day. I knew he had had enough with me. I mean, that wasn't my first dance with him. I had been sent to his office several times and had experienced his corporal punishment on multiple occasions. It never really worked with me because I had experienced much more severe punishment than that coming from a five-foot two-inch, fiery, Peruvian woman. My mother.

"This time, however, I knew things were going to be different. Mr. Drummond even had a different demeanor. The previous times I had been sent to the office for making fun of kids and for disrupting class. This time, though, I was there because I had cursed out the teacher. He did not take kindly to that, and, although I pleaded my case to get three licks, he quickly refused my requests. I guess he wasn't open to us working together to devise a consequence.

"'No,' he sternly answered. 'I am tired of seeing you in my office. The paddlings do not work. You keep coming in here and you also joke that your mother hits harder.'

"'*He remembered that*?' I thought to myself.

"'I remember that, Abiezer,' he continued. 'So, no need for the paddle today. No, you are going to be suspended for three days.'

"I was flabbergasted. Me suspended for three days? That shocked me, but what made matters worse was that this was also a week before school was out for summer vacation. I was going to miss the extra recess time. I was devastated, but not as much as I was going to be by what occurred next.

"My mother was called, and she quickly came to pick me up at the school. Since she had to return to work, she did not bother wasting time asking me why I had done what I did. Frankly, she didn't care. She knew that she had raised me better than that. She also knew that I was aware she expected better from me. She started out screaming. Her voice, when angry, terrified me more than any horror movie ever could. After a couple of minutes of her screaming at me, she started crying. She had reached her breaking point as well.

"Life had not been easy for her. Just three years before, her husband had run off with another woman—a woman who had lived in our house and eaten at our table, a woman my mother had helped when she had issues with immigration services. The fact that my father left her hurt my mother so much at times, I can still remember seeing her cry, pleading for his return. He didn't. They divorced, and she was left alone to deal with the repercussions of that, repercussions which included raising two boys on her own.

"Not only was she dealing with the after-effects of divorce (which, as one person once told me, linger on long after the papers are signed) but my mother was also dealing with the effects of her younger brother getting murdered in Chicago in a drug deal gone awry.

"Divorce, death, and now my drama. It was no wonder that her screams went from loud, angry chastisements to cries of disappointment and pain. My mother started to cry uncontrollably, and I honestly did not know what to do. A few minutes after my mother started crying, she hit the floor and passed out.

"I was scared. I had never seen anybody pass out. My first inclination was that my mother was dead. Immediately, I started crying and hit the floor on my knees pleading with God, apologizing for my actions and begging Him not to let her die. If that had happened, it would have been equivalent to the world losing the sun. My light would have been gone forever. There was no way I could have conceived surviving that.

"My mother did not die that afternoon, thank God. However, a part of me started to—the part that wished things were better for me, the part that selfishly wanted toys and other things that my mother could not afford, the part that did not think how my actions and their consequences affected her.

"That day, I finally understood that I had to make a change . . . if not for me, then for my mother. I did not want to cause her any more pain or suffering. I did not want to be the reason my mother kept shedding tears. I wanted to be good for her. I wanted to succeed for her. I wanted to make something of myself so she would be happy and know, without a shadow of a doubt, that her hard work had not been in vain."

- A.C. Cristales

Family is what brings out the essence of life. Perhaps you do not have the same type of relationship with your family that we do, but we are fairly certain that you do have *someone* who has been with you through moments of adversity. If not, perhaps you have been the family member or friend who has been there for someone else when they needed you. In either case, because of these relationships you can understand the ties we have spoken about in this course. Please take a moment to reflect upon these bonds and just how important the people with whom you have built them truly are to you.

We are very fortunate to receive the provisions we are blessed with in this life, especially the provision of people who come out of nowhere like angels sent from above. Remember, family is not always about blood. Family is also about the people in your life who accept you for who you are, who love you unconditionally and would do anything for you, even if they are not blood relations. These people, too, are members of your family.

True friends and family members, those who will remain by your side at all times, may be hard to find, but they *are* there. Seek them out. Also learn to be one yourself. Remember what we have shared about false and self-serving relationships, those that are one-sided and focus more on taking than giving. Avoid wasting your time investing either your energy or your heart in them. Avoid being the root of them as well.

We will close this course with some quotes on family that we feel reflect back on some of the truths we have shared. Before we do, however, allow us to also encourage you to be thankful for those people who have done things for you without expecting anything in return. Treasure them because they are one of life's greatest gifts to you.

May you recognize who these individuals are and express your words of gratitude to them without restraint. Tell them now, before it is too late. None of us is promised another day, and these expressions of love are too precious to waste.

Now as you move on to the next lesson, we leave you with some parting thoughts that have helped shine a light on the importance of family.

"This is part of what family is about, not just love. It's knowing that your family will be there watching out for you. Nothing else will give you that. Not money. Not fame. Not work."

- Mitch Albom

"Without a family, man, alone in the world, trembles with the cold."

- Andre Maurois

"Lots of people want to ride with you in the limo, but what you want is someone who will

take the bus with you when the limo breaks down."

- Oprah Winfrey

Family 101
Questions for Reflection

1. Think of the people who are dearest to your heart. Who are they, and why are these people so special to you? How have they added value to your life? Do you believe you have also added value to theirs? In what ways?

2. Can you identify times when your relationships with others hindered you from either seeking after or achieving goals you had set for yourself? Describe what happened and how the relationship in question adversely affected you. Look back, what would you have done differently to bring about a better result?

3. Scripture says, "Above all things, guard your heart." (Proverbs 4:23) How successfully have you done this throughout your life? How have you done so or failed to do so, and what have the results of this been? How can you guard your heart more fastidiously from this point forward?

4. Describe a time when a family member (whether they were a blood relative or not) was there for you. Be as specific as you can. How did this experience make you feel? What did it teach you?

5. In what ways can you express greater love and admiration to those who mean the world to you? Will you commit to doing this now? If so, how will you get started?

Wisdom 101

Course Description

Everyone struggles against adversity, but not everyone emerges from their struggles victoriously. Sadly, there *are* times when our challenges get the better of us. In itself, this does not constitute failure. We only fail if we refuse to learn from these moments of defeat and apply the lessons we garner in the future. This is the essence of wisdom. Those who embrace it quickly realize that it is more precious than gold.

If you apply wisdom as you proceed along your journey through life, it will reap a greater return for your future than you can possible imagine. Will you move beyond the mistakes and failures of your past, taking time to learn from them—as well as those of others who have battled through adversity and are willing to share their experiences with you—or will you instead choose to embrace failure because you refuse the blessing of insight?

A distinguished writer and historian by the name of Daniel Boorstin once wrote, "The greatest obstacle to discovery is not ignorance; it is the illusion of knowledge." Have you ever met someone who talked a great deal but in reality said very little? Some people seem to believe that the more they speak, the more capable and convincing they become. Nothing could be further from the truth. If we lack understanding or purpose, neither our word count nor the sophistication of our vocabulary can mask this.

Another trap we can fall into lies on the other end of this spectrum. If we believe we have nothing left to learn, we actually demonstrate another form of ignorance. When we become so satisfied with our own views and opinions that we refuse to entertain those of others, we likewise refuse the knowledge and wisdom they can impart to us. In their song "City of Blinding Lights," U2 sums up this concept well, saying, "The more you see, the less you know."

While the acquisition of knowledge is a wonderful thing, being able to discern what is right and true, being insightful, and simply having common sense are even greater. Deeper knowledge allows us to overcome ignorance; applied intelligence can assist us in improving the situations we may find ourselves in. But knowledge is not enough. We must also be able to relate our circumstances to the choices we have made in order to uncover their causes and avoid repeating any errors in judgment we have acted upon. This is wisdom.

"I love playing Chess. I taught myself how to play. Although I've lost more games than I've won (actually the only person I ever seem to win against is my 9-year-old son) over the years, I've gotten better. With every loss, every dumb move, I've internalized a database of strategies. I have a DVR of patterns stored in my brain. At some point, when I'm playing against a higher-caliber opponent, I will be able to draw from these memories and choose my next move in the hopes of closing in on a checkmate. You see, intelligence is knowing how to *play* the game. Wisdom is knowing which moves to make and which to avoid in order to *win* the game.

"It seems to me that the longer we live, the more aware we become of our ignorance and just how much we still

have to learn. In my opinion, that's exactly the way it should be."

- Axel Cristales

Although many people may believe otherwise, no one is born with wisdom. We are born with the capacity to think, but wisdom is not inherited. It is not something passed down from generation to generation; we cannot impart to our children only through their genetic makeup. Wisdom is the insight we gain as we learn from the mistakes we commit. It is only through our experiences—whether they have been encouraging or daunting—that we begin attaining wisdom.

My brother and I have made many mistakes throughout our lives, and we are thankful for each one. The knowledge we have gained through them has enhanced our lives immensely. Through the experiences we have endured, many of which we endured together, we have accrued the necessary knowledge to avoid repeatedly making ignorant decisions.

We shun ignorance and invite wisdom into our lives because we recognize our potential and realize that we can use the events of our past to teach others and help them reach their potential as well. There is no point in having wisdom if a person is not willing to share its blessings. We are writing this book and revealing some of the most challenging moments of our lives because we believe the knowledge we have gained through our experiences truly can be of benefit to those willing to gain from them.

There is no ego or pride involved as we do this, not even when we relate our accomplishments or the faith we have in ourselves or our purpose. We share nothing with you in order to brag or boast. One of our favorite proverbs from Scriptures says, "He who walks with the wise grows wise, but a companion of fools suffers harm." This is the sole reason that we write and speak to others as we do.

This is also why we try so diligently to stress the benefits of surrounding ourselves with people who have endured and learned from their struggles. Our spirits are fed through our environments. Consciously or unconsciously our minds absorb the thoughts and words expressed by those we associate with. Be they positive or negative, they *will* have an influence on our decision making and how we live thereafter.

To help illustrate how this is possible, let us share a story we once heard about an eagle that thought it was a chicken.

"An eaglet fell from his nest. Though he landed safely, he had no means of returning there. A boy found him lying on the ground, so he picked him up, and took him to his father's farm where he placed him among the chickens. Since they were the only models he had on which to base his own behavior, in time the eaglet began imitating them. He learned to cluck and scratch the dirt looking for worms just like they did. Then one day, when he furiously flapped his wings as he had seen some of his brothers do, he flew a few feet in the air before crashing back down to the earth.

"For a moment, he was intrigued by the possibilities this new experience offered—that is, until his brothers laughed at him and told him he was crazy for thinking he could fly. Rather than continuing to follow his dream

and attempting to prove them wrong, the eaglet went right back to digging in the dirt.

"Sometime later, once he was fully grown, the former eaglet looked up in the sky and saw a bird soaring majestically and with ease across the sky.

"'What's that?' he asked.

"'That's an eagle,' some of his brethren replied. 'They're birds of the air while we're birds of the ground.'

"And sadly that's exactly where the eagle remained. Because he chose to think like a chicken, he buried his true nature within him."

The obvious moral of this story is that if you want to fly like an eagle, then you cannot get your counsel from chickens. Whether it is through reading books about people who have faced adversity and survived, listening to speakers who have known success after failure, or simply talking to people who have lived through trying times, let your mind be influenced by positive thinkers. Be very cautious of the environment you put yourself in because the influence it can have on you is powerful. The people who populate it can either serve you by providing encouragement through your trials or, if you allow them to do so, can wear you down so badly that they break your spirit and ultimately steal your potential for success.

Acquiring wisdom may take time, but fortunately it can be gained through virtually any medium. In our own lives, we have primarily grown in this area through three different avenues: listening, learning, and losing.

One of the things we enjoy doing most is getting together at family functions and sitting around uncles and aunts who are much older than us. We get a charge from their talks, listening to their pearls of wisdom. Their stories make ours relevant because we understand that they are all woven together, the common thread among them being pain caused by suffering through adverse times. Such are other stories from other people's experiences. We may not all live the same life, we may not all grow up in the same neighborhoods, and our economic statuses may be different, but one thing we all do share is that we have all been hurt at one time or another. We encourage you to listen and let other people's scars speak to yours.

We believe we were great educators not because we were enthusiastic about leading, but rather because we were enthusiastic about learning. We love to learn. In fact, we love the process even more than the actual product. We get excited about the journey from foolishness to wisdom, and this excitement leads us to engage in activities that can further our purpose and advance our journey. We read a great deal. We study notable men and women who have accomplished great things through their resiliency. We always try to take something away from every encounter we have with people. We encourage you to be similarly receptive. Be willing to fill your cup with the wisdom of others so that when you are faced with a difficult situation, you have a wealth of experience to draw from.

In all honesty, we have lost more times than we have won when facing adversity. But, to be equally honest, because of this we have also gained much more than we otherwise would have if we been allowed to become complacent with victory. From our point of view, each defeat has carried with it a lesson and each failure has remained a challenge yet to be conquered. Through the acquisition and application of wisdom, we believe they can be.

We make failure either temporary or permanent through our response to it, through our decision to learn from it or not. Whether it is a failed marriage, a bankrupt business, or an unsuccessful idea, lessons for the future can be drawn from every missed opportunity. We encourage you to seek out those lessons and apply them in your life as you move forward toward your goals. We would also remind you that there is power to be found in sharing your story with others. Seek to inspire others by relating your experiences to them. Failure is more certain than success in life, and people want someone they can relate to when confronting it. Help others overcome their present challenges and you will begin to rise above the shortcomings of your own past.

"One of my first major keynote addresses was entitled, 'Be Strong. Be Courageous. Be You.' For the first forty minutes, I took an audience of over three hundred high school students on a

personal journey detailing what it meant to be strong, courageous, and authentic. In closing, however, I dropped a bomb on them. I told them that my life had not always been characterized by those three traits. My exact words to them were, 'I haven't always been mentally strong. I haven't always been courageous enough to do the right thing. I haven't always been myself. Yes, I've tried to copy and be like others.'

"In sharing that, I was able to show them that just because I was extolling those three attributes, it didn't mean that they had always been present in my life. I wanted them to be able to take joy in knowing that none of us starts out like that. And it's true. None of us begins our college lives, our careers, our marriages, or our parenting knowing all the answers. There will be times of great learning, and this will come either through study or through failure.

"As I continued, I also told them, 'Yes, I messed up while I was a student. You see before you a person who, at twenty-four years old, was already a leader on a campus in the one of the largest school districts in Texas. However, don't fail to also see the thirteen-year-old who was suspended from school on several occasions for cussing out his teachers. You see before you a person who graduated high school in three years and had his Master's degree by twenty-three. However, don't fail to also see the kid who had suicidal thoughts because he did not know how his life was going to get better. You see before you a person who uses his own rap music as a means to hook and engage his audience. However, don't fail to also see the major reasons why I started writing songs. That was my way of venting frustration about my family life, my way of overcoming being ostracized because I was no longer following the path my friends were taking, and, most importantly, my opportunity to share my voice with the world.

"I didn't always have all the answers. In my foolishness, I actually believed I knew what I was doing and that even if I did get into trouble, it was only going to affect me anyway. I had to hit my lowest points and witness the pain I was causing those around me in order to know it was time for a change.

"That is when I began to seek out wisdom. I wanted to be better, but I didn't know how to go about doing so. How was I to become a better student? How was I to change what was being written about me? I had to look for answers to those questions if I wanted to see any significant change. That was when wisdom became my sister and understanding my relative. Through wisdom, I learned that there are things in life I would never have control over

but still had the power to make the best of; I learned that all my friends didn't have the best in mind for me and that in order for me to truly soar to higher heights, I had to be courageous and leave the 'chickens' 'behind.

"I have learned from my experiences. At 32, I continue to learn from them. I am proud to admit that I don't have all the answers. I am proud to admit that I am not perfect. There is freedom to be found in such honest confessions. It is not a freedom that grants you liberty to do foolish things, but rather one that comforts you in your failure, saying, 'You can rise again.'"

- A.C. Cristales

As we prepare to bring this course to a close, we would like to share with you a sample of one of the many conversations we had with our students while we were administrators. We believe the seed of this topic resides in the heart of interactions such as the one that follows.

"Do you know why your parents came to the U.S.?"

"To have a better life."

"How?"

"I don't know."

"Because here, in this country, you have opportunities that aren't given to you where your parents are from."

This exchange, or one very similar, occurred almost daily. We worked in schools where the majority of students were first-generation Hispanics, students who, as we observed them, took advantage of their parents' lack of knowledge concerning the English language, who were foolish regarding the culture of American schools, or who used their residency status as an excuse to remain uninvolved in their pursuit of a better education.

These students misbehaved because they thought the little knowledge they had and their parents lacked granted them "get out of jail free" cards. They did not recognize that knowledge is only real, is only powerful, when it is applied to make our circumstances better. As we explained at the outset of this course, this is the heart of wisdom . . . and that is exactly what these parents displayed struggling to create better opportunities for their children than those they had for themselves.

As two men who had walked in their shoes and been the recipients of the same kind of love from their own mother and father, it always frustrated us when these students disregarded and disrespected their parents' struggles to create a better life for them. Working in schools, the saddest thing we encountered was witnessing how many students seemed to undervalue their education and, in turn, diminish their future worth because of their inability to recognize the importance of wisdom.

Our mother was no different than the parents of those students. We can still hear her saying to us, *"Si yo tuviera educacion, yo seria mas."* These words meant, "If I had an education, I would be so much more." She may not have had a great deal of formal education, but what she did have was wisdom—and this she had in abundance. She had gained valuable life experience from the mistakes of her past, and she taught the lessons she had learned to us.

As we mentioned earlier, wisdom cannot simply be passed on from generation to generation. We do not inherit the wealth of experience and knowledge our parents possess simply because we carry their genes. No, we must make a conscious and active decision to do so. The lessons our mother shared with us were the greatest form of education we ever received, taught by the greatest teacher we have ever known. Our students did not always see this in their relationships with their own parents. We urge you to demonstrate wisdom, to learn from their failure in this area and cling to those who are willing bestow the wealth of their experiences upon you.

Remember, wisdom is not meant to be hoarded, it is meant to be passed on. Ignorance can be fatal, but wisdom—the ability *today* to see *tomorrow* because of *yesterday*—is a fountain from which the blessings of experience freely flow. May you seize them and integrate them for your own lives so you can then pass them on and, in so doing, become vessels of knowledge for others as well.

Wisdom 101
Questions for Reflection

1. "If I had known then, what I know now . . ." is a powerful statement. What thoughts or experiences come to mind when you read that phrase? Can you identify a point in your life when you have said these words yourself? What knowledge could a younger version of yourself have used during that time, and how would such wisdom had made a difference?

2. Take a moment to reflect on the company you keep. Is the environment you place yourself in positive and conducive to helping you fulfill your goals? Who have been the primary sources of wisdom to this point in your life? Has the information they have shared helped you more than hindered you or vise versa? Are there other founts of wisdom you could or should look to? Who might they be?

3. In what way(s) do you acquire wisdom? How do you feed your heart, mind, and soul in this regard?

4. Wisdom means that you are constantly learning. What are some things you know you must learn in order to better prepare you to fulfill your destiny? How will you go about acquiring this knowledge? How will you apply it once you do?

5. Even if you have doubts, you, too, have wisdom to impart to others. Identify two or three lessons you have learned in your life that you can share with the world. Record them, and identify the people you think most need to know them. How will you go about sharing your wisdom with them?

Greatness 101

Course Description

Every man, woman, and child on this planet has a purpose. Part of that purpose is to change the world for the better. While this may seem like an extreme statement, it is true nevertheless. In some way, each and every one of us has the potential to make a difference—how much of an impact we have depends solely on how much we believe in our ability to do so.

Do not settle for a lifetime of mediocrity. Commit yourself instead to greatness, no matter the cost. Are you willing to surrender yourself to the truth that you were meant to do extraordinary things in the time that you have been granted? Will you dare to believe in your ability to change the world, one relationship at a time, or will your lack of such faith instead leave you simply another face in the crowd? Both this generation and those that follow will be affected your response.

Socrates, one of the great Greek philosophers, once said, "The unexamined life is not worth living." We agree. At some point, we all must experience a moment of self-assessment, a moment when we explore who we are and what we have accomplished throughout our years on this planet. We do not need to fear such appraisals, even if we have fallen short of the goals we have hoped to achieve. This type of examination is not of the pass or fail variety, but rather is an honest evaluation of where we currently stand versus where we still hope to be. The greatest and most liberating aspect of such an assessment is that our life stories are still being written as long as our hearts continue beating and our lungs continue drawing breath. Once we strip away any doubt and uncertainty, any fear or shame, we set ourselves free to move on and continue pursuing the greatness that dwells inside each one of us.

"A lot has changed in the world since I was a teenager. Social media has taken center stage in the lives of most people. Smart phones seem to be everywhere. Books are becoming a thing of the past because vast storehouses of knowledge are just a click away on the Internet. As much as things have changed, however, many things have also stayed the same.

"When I talk personally to high school students, I always get the same impression—they're all looking for some sort of identity. The truth is, many adults are still doing the same. There seems to be a popular misconception that once someone turns twenty-one, or graduates from college, or gets married, he or she knows who he or she is. But that is not always true. Sometimes we turn twenty-one and still have no clue what we want out of life. Sometimes we graduate from college and still do not know what we want to do. Sometimes we get married and still have little idea how deeply affecting relationships with others can be.

"Reaching a milestone doesn't necessarily mean that we know who we are. The way to truly know who we are is to examine ourselves. I do that on a daily basis."

- A.C. Cristales

With this in mind we would like to ask a question.

Who are you?

When you look in the mirror, what type of man or woman do you see? What is it that you want to achieve in life? Do you believe that the potential for greatness dwells within you? Think back to the story of the eagle in the previous chapter. He was born with the greatness of a mighty bird inside of him. He had powerful wings that would have enabled him to soar mightily through the sky and rise above the clouds when storms came. He had exceptional vision that would have granted him a more beautiful view of the world that the one he had grown accustomed to. Myriad possibilities were within his reach, but instead of making his nest near the heavens, he instead dwelt among lesser birds on the ground. But none of this mattered as long as the eagle was blind to it. So it is with us. Our greatness rest upon how and what we think of ourselves as well.

Sadly, many people examine their lives only when they find themselves in a rut or when they have hit rock bottom. We cannot gauge our potential accurately in such situations. Although we may have nowhere to go but up, we are often so busy focusing on the valley we find ourselves in that we fail to see the paths leading out of it. That is a difficult position to be in to be sure, but it is a position of our own making as well.

My brother and I have placed ourselves in many situations without first considering if they were truly where we wanted to be or offered what we really wanted. Because we failed to ask ourselves if they were going to be beneficial to us in the long run—because we leapt before we looked, so to speak—we have jumped into things and failed to realize, until it was too late to change course, that where we were going to land was actually taking us further away from our goals. Because of this, we have needlessly wasted time and energy that could have been spent much more wisely fulfilling our dreams.

There is great danger in neglecting to consider whether or not the things we choose to pursue truly conform to who we are and what we want out of life. The greater danger, however, is not understanding our potential. A lack of identity brings with it a lack of judgment. Foolish choices are minimized when we know who we are and what we are capable of doing.

One of our favorite quotes is by the great Abraham Lincoln. He said, "Every man is born an original, but sadly, most men die copies." In studying the lives of great men and women throughout history, individuals who have left great legacies, we have discovered that their greatness was in large part dependent upon their individuality.

"Just recently I decided to leave my position as a principal because I felt that I wasn't living up to my potential. While the decision to finally act came only a short time ago, the actual thought came several years back. It was a Monday afternoon in 2008 after I was called to attend a meeting with several other school administrators. I'd been an educator for almost ten years at that time.

"Coming out of college, I knew I wanted to do something honorable, something that would help people and, more specifically, something that would help at-risk children. I taught for three years

before falling into the trap of believing that I needed to become a principal if I wanted to make the changes I thought our educational system needed, changes that would benefit all children, not just one group. I use the word 'trap' because in the eight years that I served as a school administrator, I never felt the same sense of accomplishment that I did while I was teaching. I was an individual the students admired and looked up to. I had built my nest among those small souls hoping they, too, would one day aspire to reach new heights. There were thousands of teachers throughout this country, but in the eyes of my students, I was the only one that mattered. Leaving them in that capacity was difficult.

"During my first three years of teaching, I dedicated myself to becoming an assistant principal, and I met that goal. Even after meeting the necessary requirements, however, I still faced a number of hurdles, namely people who didn't believe in me and felt that I needed more time in the classroom before becoming an administrator. I understood that perhaps they believed a leader must first learn to follow others before he can expect others to follow him, and I respected that opinion. But I also understood the viewpoint of Harold R. McAlindon, considered to be one of the top management speakers in America, when he wrote, 'Do not follow where the path may lead. Go instead where there is no path and leave a trail.' I considered myself to be a trailblazer even then, just as I do today. I felt that my ability to forge my own way would not only establish new trails others could follow on their own paths of success, but also open doors for me on my way to becoming a principal. My ascent, however, was not as smooth as I had hoped it would be.

"Fortunately, God has a sovereign way of setting events in motion that will bring us to the places He desires us to be. After all, God is a hunter and destiny, His trap. When He wants us, He'll get us; where He wants us, He'll put us. God brought many people into my life He then used to lead me to my destined place, people whose influence helped shape my thinking in a positive way. Of course the naysayers remained, but their voices became less and less prominent against the chorus of those providing encouragement. Every person I encountered, supportive or otherwise, and every situation I experienced, promising and challenging alike, served a purpose on my path to greater things.

"Still, I was not content with being merely an assistant principal because I knew I had the ability to do so much more. Throughout my years in the district, I had been given leadership responsibilities, but they did not satisfy my hunger for more. I wanted to rise to the position of principal very much. I was hoping that it would fulfill me. During that Monday meeting, however, I observed the people who had been promoted before me, and I came to the realization that I was settling for less than what I deserved. I didn't see myself as one of the 250 administrators in the school district, but rather as an individual with much more to offer not only my colleagues and students, but also the world.

"I would like to say that I made the decision to leave in pursuit of what I saw as my greater purpose that very day. Instead it took five more years for me to do so, sitting in another meeting with other principals just as I had all those years before. That was when the revelation that I wanted to be a writer finally overtook me. I wanted to kiss the sky, but in order to do that I needed to shed myself of the fear that was holding me hostage and find the courage to

break free. I was able to do so because I placed power into my thoughts."

- Axel Cristales

Sometimes we remain at jobs we dread simply because they pay the bills. Sometimes we remain in unfulfilling relationships simply because we find companionship, even with unhappy partners, preferable to loneliness. While remaining idle in such a manner may feel safe, in reality we are doing nothing more than squandering who we could be and what we could be achieving if only we put forth the effort. We all need a catalyst that will get us on course to greater things in our lives, especially if we remaining idle is leaving us mired in mediocrity.

"'I'm thinking of doing more motivational speaking presentations,' I said.

"'Really?' the director I was speaking to replied. 'That's great. I know a guy in South Texas, a superintendent, who does motivational speaking on the side. He also raps when he speaks. You

probably can't do that. But yes, you should pursue more motivational speaking opportunities.'

"'You probably can't do that.'

"'*Amazing*,' I thought. '*Crazy*.' Who was this guy to tell me what I could or could not do? I know it probably wasn't his intention to be discouraging, but I distinctly remember walking out of his office smirking, nodding my head and saying to myself, '*This guy doesn't know me. He'll see one day what I can and cannot do*.'

"His ignorance of what I could do, of the potential that dwelt within me, has been the fuel I have needed to keep the spark ablaze as I have pursued my dreams and followed my own path to greatness . . . that the greatness I know I am destined for."

- A.C. Cristales

The most unfulfilling times my brother and I have personally experienced have been those when we have sat around being unproductive. Although we expect great things to happen in and evolve from our lives, the reality is that we must work hard to see them come to pass. When we have neglected to do that, only disappointment, in ourselves and in our situations, resulted.

John Maxwell, an American pastor, author, and speaker said, "Disappointment is the gap between reality and what is expected." Have you ever found yourself disappointed with your situation? Ever wished for more out of life? Ever longed for a better and brighter tomorrow? Are you perhaps feeling any of these things now? If you can answer any of these questions in the affirmative, we encourage you to stop right this minute, look very deeply into your life, into your heart, and ask yourself why. The answer to this question truly does rest within you; it is something only you can identify for yourself.

If you lack fulfillment, if you envision yourself going one direction when your life is going another, perhaps it is because you have settled for less than your best. Perhaps you are suppressing your potential because you are doing what someone else *thought* you could do instead of doing what you *knew* you could do. Only you have the power to change this. The good news is, you can do so at any time. As we have mentioned before, as long as you are still alive, it is never too late to change the course of your life. Do you want to fly? Then you need to decide right here and right now how high.

As you pursue this goal, we would like to remind you of three important truths and encourage you to let them guide you as you strive to unleash the greatness within you.

1. You must stay true to being an original.
2. You must stay true to your abilities and values.
3. You must stay true to the truth.

"No one can take your place. Realize this and be yourself. You have no obligation to succeed. You have only the obligation to be true to yourself."

- Og Mandino

The world has an estimated population of 7.115 billion people, but you are unique among them all. Others may have grown up in the same environment, but you saw and processed things differently from anyone else. Your experiences make you an original. As similar as my brother and I are, we look at things differently because we have different personalities. Although we lived through many of the same circumstances, they affected us differently and defined our personalities in singular ways. That is the beauty of our relationship. The variety of our individual lives enhances the spirit of both. It is no different for you. You may have friends you have known your entire life or family members you have experienced virtually every milestone with, but none of these people will share all of the customs or values you have adopted.

Be true to yourself, not to someone else. Lasting success lies in being authentic. Do not waste your time and energy trying to imitate others. You will never be happy and you will never know true achievement if you do.

"I love Jordan brand shoes. Growing up I remember always wanting some. Right before the start of my sixth-grade school year, my mom finally bought me a pair. I was the happiest kid in the world at that moment. I am pretty sure I grabbed a basketball that very day and started practicing my fade away jumper. I am sure that I even dunked a basketball that day. Plain and simple, my Jordans made me feel like I could fly.

"Eighteen years later, Jordans are still selling strong, topping one billion dollars in annual revenue. SportsOneSource.com, a retail tracking firm for the sports market, reports that three out of every four pairs of basketball shoes sold in the United States are Jordans. Michael Jordan has not played a game in the NBA in over ten years, but his brand is still in high demand. With such a high demand, imitators have risen up trying to cash in on his fame as well. These imitation

Jordans look like the original, but they are not. Although they may be cheaper to buy, that doesn't make them better or even equal to the real thing. The savings come at a cost—comfort and quality.

"Don't devalue yourself by becoming an imitation of someone else. Be an original, just as you were meant to be. You will never be comfortable in your own skin and you will never rise to the heights that are possible for you if you do anything less."

- A.C. Cristales

You have been bestowed with talents, gifts, and ideas no one else in this world but you can share. You have stories and life experiences only you can relate to others. Use these things to set yourself apart and demonstrate the potential for greatness dwelling within you. A light has been given to each one of us, the value of which is determined by how brightly we let it shine and how far we make it reach. We challenge you to let your unique light shine wherever you may find yourself. Let it shine upon those around you and illuminate new possibilities for them as you blaze new trials they can follow.

"It's not hard to make decisions when you know what your values are."

- Roy Disney

"After working in public education for more than 10 years, I had the following conversations with students on many occasions.

"'Why did you do that?'

"'Because.'

"'Because why?'

"'Because he told me to.'

"'Because he told you to, huh?'

"'Yes.'

"'So, if I take you to the top of the roof of this school and tell you to jump, you're going to do it?'

"'No.'

"'They why would you do what he told you to do. Does he have that much power over you?'

"'I don't know.'

"I have used those final three words when answering somebody and it has greatly frustrated them. That phrase seems to have the same effect on most people. While it's not always negative to not know something, there are some things we *must* know. One, as we have already discussed, is that we must know who we are. We must also know what we value. Gandhi, once said, 'Values become your destiny.' Under this philosophy, we become what we esteem and, by virtue of this, what we invest our time in.

"I know it's easier for some people to put on a mask and pretend to be someone they are not for fear of being ostracized, mocked, and criticized, but there is no liberty in that. There is freedom in being we who are and in honestly representing those things we value in our daily walk. We don't have to be perfect; it isn't about that. It is about being transparent.

"You will win the respect of more people by being who you truly are than by pretending to be someone you are not, by standing fast to what you believe in than by being a moral chameleon. Never let others tell you who to be, or what you should value. There is nothing to gain in doing so, but rather everything to lose."

- A.C. Cristales

"Then you will know the truth and the truth shall set you free."

(John 8:32)

The truth, and nothing but the truth, is that you were born with the potential for greatness already inside of you. You were created and put on this earth for a given purpose.

To this point, perhaps you have known only hardship and trial. Perhaps you have suffered loss or failed to yet find true satisfaction in your accomplishments. Perhaps you have allowed your past or even current mistakes to impair how you see yourself and gauge your self-worth. Whatever condition you find yourself in, whatever circumstances may surround you, do NOT allow anything save truth to define you. And the truth is, you are more powerful than you give yourself credit for.

R.H. Macy opened four retail stores between 1843 and 1855, all of which failed. Today, there exist over 780 Macy's department stores. Dr. Seuss's first book, *To Think That I Saw It on Mulberry Street*, was rejected by 27 different publishers. Today, nearly every child has read at least one of his many works. Thomas Edison was told by his teachers he was too stupid to learn anything. He went on to establish 2,332 patents worldwide, over one thousand of which were in the United States alone. You may have experienced failure throughout your life, but *you* are not a failure. Just as was true with these men, there is greatness inside of you as well.

Allow yourself to discover something you feel passionately about and let that become the foundation of your dreams, of your future success. As you pursue these things, remember that nothing of value ever comes easily. Trash can be thrown together in minutes, but masterpieces take time. Sometimes we must go through several rehearsals or experience multiple setbacks before our final goals are achieved. Push through the challenges that rise up against you and emerge victorious, stronger having endured them than you ever could have been had you not. You are an original and greatness lives inside of you.

Believe this. Build on it and live like it. Let nothing stand in your way on your path to a better life.

Greatness 101
Questions for Reflection

1. Up to this point in your life, what has been the fuel that has driven you to succeed, the motivating factor that has refused to let you give up even when circumstances became challenging? How can you continue to make use of the in order to draw from this in order to soar to even greater heights? If such a source of inspiration has been lacking in your life, how do you think you can change this? Where, or to whom, can you begin looking to today to find this?

2. Why do you think people experience disappointment when they are not doing something they feel passionately about and believe they are called to do? Do you think we can ever experience true satisfaction in life if we choose to live in such a manner? Explain why or why not.

3. To build upon the last question, are you satisfied with the things you have achieved thus far? Examine your life honestly, as Socrates urges us to do. Are you currently striving for greatness or are

you settling for mediocrity? If you are not content with your current situation and the level of success you have achieved, what can do to change them?

4. Do you consider yourself to be an original, or do you instead mimic the identities of others? If you chose the former, explain how you believe you stand out from others in the crowd. If you chose the latter, do you believe that a change may necessary after reading this chapter? How can you bring such change about?

5. What is one truth you will repeat on a daily basis to remind yourself that the potential and capability for greatness already dwell within you? Do not simply say this truth aloud. Write it down and post it in prominent places so you will be sure to see it and be reminded of it every day.

Time 101

Course Description

It is impossible for anyone to determine the exact moment his or her last breath will be drawn, but one thing is certain— eventually time *will* run out for us all. Because of this, we dare not take even one second for granted. We should instead invest our time wisely, using it to make our mark on the world and to gain the greatest return possible on the days we have been allotted.

Time is fleeting, but it is also a tremendous gift. How much you value the time available to you now will determine how much you are able to accomplish in the future. Will you resolve to make the most of this gift, choosing to live every day to its fullest, or will you instead squander it and, in the end, blame it for everything you could have done if only a few more years had been available to you?

In the book of James, life is described as being like a vapor, something that exists only for a moment, then disappears. It may be frightening to view our lives in such a manner, but what my brother and I believe to be even more frightening is how people will account for the time that was given to them once their days are done.

God grants each of us only a limited amount of time to do what He has purposed in our hearts to accomplish. Some of us may be born on the wrong side of the tracks; some may be discriminated against because of who we are or what we believe; we may not all be the brightest colors in the box. Despite any of this, God still loves us all equally, enough to give everyone the same amount of time each day—24 hours, 1440 minutes, 86,400 seconds. What we do with this commodity, one of the most precious of all His blessings, is of great importance. Whether we use it or allow it be wasted, not even one second can be carried over from one day to the next. Yesterday is not today, and today will not be tomorrow. This is why we must make the most of the time given to us right now.

"Twenty-four hours. That's how much time you have been given today. It does not matter if you're Caucasian, African-American, Hispanic, or Asian; time does not provide any race or ethnic group more advantages or disadvantages than any other. It is simply opportunity, and

it is given to us the moment we wake up. It is entirely up to us how we will respond. Will we make the most of it or squander it . . . those are really our only choices. We can either maximize to the fullest extent the precious hours and minutes that make up today or waste them, plain and simple.

"I have to admit that I used to hate waking up early. I loathed it, in fact. The thought of getting up, taking a shower, and ironing my clothes for the day didn't exactly bring euphoric feelings for me. That, in turn, made me a very grumpy person on most mornings.

"Now, I've actually grown quite fond of waking up early. In fact, most weekdays I am up at four o'clock in the morning. It may take me ten or fifteen minutes to get going, but at the very least I am awake. Why the change? When I truly realized that being blessed to wake up another morning was not something I should take for granted, there was nothing else I could do. Knowing that once the alarm on my iPhone goes off I can wake up and get started on my day excites me. I now recognize that time cannot be wasted, that after each day is over, that is it. We will not be able to retrieve a single one, so we should make the most of them while we have them.

"I am not urging you to start waking up at four o'clock. However, I am encouraging you to allow a feeling of gratitude, a thankfulness that you are alive, to overtake you every morning that you wake up. You have been given another twenty-four hours to do something phenomenal. A new day has arrived and with it comes new opportunities. Make the most of it."

- A.C. Cristales

Ordinary people think about taking action and claiming brighter futures but go no further;

extraordinary people go the extra mile and actually act upon those thoughts. Which type of person are you?

Do you have things you want to accomplish in your life? Do you have aspirations you know will take time and energy to see fulfilled? Do you have dreams you long to see come true? None of these things will happen on their own. If you have desires that still remain unrealized, you cannot allow fear, doubt, or laziness to steal even one more second from you. Instead, set your goals, determine the steps you will need to take in order to reach them, and get to work. Time is the only thing of value that we really own. Treat it like the gift it is.

> **"Speak to a first-generation college student who has failed to put forth the required effort and been placed on academic probation his freshman year in college, and you will learn the value of one *year*.**

> **"Speak to a mother who has held her premature baby in her arms, and you will learn the value of one *month*.**

"Speak to the high school football coach and his players after they have lost the 'big game' and you will learn the value of one *week*.

"Speak to anyone who has lost his or her job but still has three mouths to feed, and you'll learn the value of one *day*.

"Speak to the hopeful lover who has waited to meet the woman he loves, and you'll learn the value of one *hour*.

"Speak to the person who has missed his or her flight, train, or bus, and you'll learn the value of one *minute*.

"Speak to anyone who has swerved in the opposite direction to avoid a car accident, and you'll learn the value of one *second*.

"No matter how brief it may be, any amount of time is precious and has the

power to make a real difference in our lives."

- Axel Cristales

As we mentioned in the previous chapter, greatness is bred through the power of thought. It is nurtured through knowing the importance of time. Achieving greatness takes more than simply dreams and plans. While these things are vital as they give us hope, the incentive to press on when challenges arise, and the tools with which to meet them, we should not commit ourselves to them more than the actual effort required to see them to fruition. We must avoid setting our eyes on tomorrow alone when there are concerns and battles to fight today. For this reason, we must be warriors, fighting in the present for what we hope to be and do in the future.

"Take it from someone who waited and waited to leave the security of his job in pursuit of his dreams to become a writer—there's a reason why it's called fleeting time. Once we let it fly by, we can never catch it again.

"I waited a long time for things to line up just right. I wanted my checking account to have just the right amount of money in it to sustain me; I wanted my children to be the right ages so that they could understand. But as the days turned into weeks and weeks into years, I began to recognize that there comes a point when saying, 'I'll do it tomorrow" becomes an excuse that can quickly and easily turn into regret. At some point we just have to figure out for ourselves what matters most to us and we have to get after it.

"The longer we wait to go in search of our destinies, the less likely we are to find them. Napoleon Hill, an American author in the field of personal success, wrote, 'Do not wait; the time will never be just right. Start where you stand and work whatever tools you may have at your command, and better tools will be found as you go along.' As I've embarked upon this new journey, I've had to kick some old habits. I've had to spend more time reading and learning about the writing craft and less on social media, more time writing and less watching television, more time being faithful and less being stressed. I've gained new tools in doing so.

"If there's one thing that I've learned on this new journey, it is that time can be the greatest ally for those whose thoughts produce a positive attitude. It's only the negative thinkers who complain that there is not enough time for them to do anything. Woe to them, I say. They just don't know the score."

- Axel Cristales

Not one person has a "mountaintop experience" and stays there forever. As we mentioned at the beginning of this book, life is a rollercoaster ride that is always plunging, ascending, then plunging again. So many people fail to see the reality that we all suffer, all cry, all have questions why we may face seemingly overwhelming odds at times and are left wonder when will things get better. We do this because we fixate on the past and allow it to become an anchor holding us back. We live crucified upon the crosses of yesterday's failures, hindering our ability to act today, to seek the opportunities that may appear before us at any given moment. We can never accomplish anything if we allow ourselves to remain prisoners of our pasts. We must instead cast off those chains, and we must do so without hesitation.

"I have shared about how my childhood and my upbringing were not all that wonderful. My father's absences had a lot to do with that. However, it boggles my mind that even though more than twenty years have passed since my father left me, the effects of his departure still linger on.

"I like to refer this as a 'thorn in my side,' a thorn that I have pleaded with God to remove on many occasions only to have Him tell me, 'No. My grace is sufficient for you.' While in my heart I know this should be comforting, this is

not quite the answer I want to hear when I am down and out, with tears rolling down my cheeks and my head filled with thoughts of unworthiness.

"What this response reveals to me, however, is that there are certain trials, certain memories, even certain consequences that will never go away. No matter how hard we may want to bury them, they will always come back and, with them, the same pain and confusion they initially wrought. Feelings like these are okay. They remind us that we are not robots, but rather human beings who live in a fallen world where no one and nothing is or ever will be perfect.

"No matter how high a status we may reach or how many accomplishments we may attain, we will never escape moments of heartache and bewilderment. But, we do not have to let these things hold us back. We can

instead choose to allow time to heal our wounds as much as possible, then learn to live with what remains and press on. That is what warriors do."

- A.C. Cristales

We know there are certain things that happen in our lives that are traumatic, events that may very well challenge a person's will to live. It is in those moments, however, that we must remember there is still time for things to improve as long as we are willing to take action and see this done. The pain of yesterday does not have to rob us of the promises of today. We urge you not to allow the heartache and pain of yesterday to keep you from learning, growing, taking risks, and being the best you can be in whatever you set your mind to.

"I've experienced painful moments other than when my father left me. One in particular was going through a divorce. I have to say that experience hit me hard. Yes, it knocked the wind out of me and completely brought me down to

the point where I could neither sleep nor function. In my mind, I was a failure, not only in my own eyes but also the eyes of those around me. What was so wrong with me that I could not make my marriage work? I lived with questions like that plaguing me and, to be honest, I allowed them to keep me from loving and trusting again.

"I would like to say that those feelings of failure and inadequacy have long since passed and no longer affect me. I can't do that, however. If I did, I would belittle the experience, and I do not want to do that. I learned a great deal from going through a divorce, therefore the feelings and memories that came with it *do* affect me. What is different now is that they do not hold me hostage. I acknowledge my failure, but I also realize the strength gained from it.

"You see, in every mistake, every failure, every defeat, I believe there is a lesson.

That is why it is fine to acknowledge our mishaps, misfortunes, and mistakes. Quite simply, they are going to happen. Danger only arises when we stop living because of them. If we stop living, we will never fulfill our God-given purposes. How many other lives will be negatively impacted if we choose to do that?

"Personally, that is not a question I want to discover the answer to. That is why I press on. In the time I have been blessed with, I am going to make a difference."

- A.C. Cristales

My brother and I have encountered many forms of derision throughout our lives, especially as we have set out to fulfill our dreams and do something we believe will be of true value to others.

"You? You're going to try to impact the world?"
"Don't you know who your father is?"

212

"Don't you know that the highest level of education your mother and father completed was elementary school?"

"Don't you realize Hispanic kids like you are not supposed to graduate from high school, let alone college, much less ones that come from a single parent home?"

"You grew up around gangs, drugs, and physical abuse. When have you known someone like you to make it through college?"

"You only know custodial work."

"You smell like your father's machine shop."

"You look like a worker on an assembly line, like your mom."

"The only people who make an impact on the world are the ones running their own companies, philanthropists who make millions and millions of dollars. That's not you. How do you think you're going to make any difference?"

As you pursue your own dreams and ambitions, some people may say similar things and ask similar questions. We encourage you to let your answer be parallel ours. Tell them that you live to make today matter.

If you maximize your time today, aligning your goals with what you can reasonably accomplish, you have the ability to do just that. Tomorrow will take care of itself. As sure as the sun rises, it will be there waiting to greet you as you step into it. Focus on today.

You may not look like the ideal candidate to make an impact through your actions, you may not even feel that you are capable of doing so. There have been times when we certainly did not. But we have. To this point in our lives, we have had the privilege of teaching wonderful students, instilling in them the values we believed were necessary to assist them in fulfilling their own dreams. We have been honored to travel around the United States and speak to a wide variety of audiences on what hope and inspiration have meant to us. We have been blessed with the ability to provide others with employment and educational opportunities. Already, we have made a difference in others' lives, and we will continue to do so because we have our wills set upon it. This has all been possible because we have learned to make the most of the time we have been given.

We encourage you to learn this lesson as well.

Yesterday you may have cried; today you can make someone laugh. Yesterday you may have wounded someone close to you; today you can ask that person for forgiveness. Yesterday someone may have discouraged you; today you can remain strong enough to encourage someone else.

In Mitch Albom's book, *The Timekeeper*, there is a character by the name of Victor who tries to outrun death when he is diagnosed with cancer. He meets a man named Dor, characterized as the father of time. Victor questions Dor as to why God limits the days men may live. Victor responds by telling him that God does this in order to make each one precious. Make this day precious. Today, do everything in your power to make life matter, both for yourself and for someone else.

There is a proverb that says, "Killing time is not murder; it's suicide." What this means is that wasting time accomplishes nothing more than also wasting opportunity. Every minute that we allow to pass idly by stifles our potential that much more. In essence, wasting time causes us to waste away as well, not to mention those who love us and believe in us. No one wants to come to the end of his or her life and reflect upon missed opportunities, realizing only too late that no time remains to do the great things he or she planned to do.

Time is precious. Make the most of every day remaining to you, remembering that none of us is promised even a minute, even a second more. Do not live to regret the chances you did not take, the opportunities you did not seize, or the choices you waited too long to make. Live your life, and live it to the fullest by making each second count.

May the following quotes we share in closing this course encourage and assist you in this endeavor.

"It is always wise to look ahead, but difficult to look further than you can see."

- Winston Churchill

"Find something you love to do so much you can't wait for the sun to rise to do it all over again."

- Chris Gardner

"Time is more valuable than money. You can get more money, but you cannot get more time."

- Jim Rohn

"Most of our lives are crucified between two thieves, yesterday and tomorrow. We never live today. But the time to live is now. It is today."

-W. Oscar Thompson

Time 101
Questions for Reflection

1. When a new day arrives, with it comes new opportunities. What are your thoughts and feelings regarding this statement? Do you agree or disagree with it? Why?

2. Do you have dreams and aspirations yet unfulfilled? Have you been planning something for the past few days, months, or even years? What are some things you can do today that will help you put into action what, to this point, have remained only thoughts? What about tomorrow? Next week? Next month? How can you begin utilizing your time in a manner that will better assist you in reaching your goals?

3. In order to accomplish the things we set out to do, we must invest your time wisely. Do you believe you invest your time wisely? On a scale of 1 to 5, with 1 being the weakest and 5 being the strongest, how would you rate yourself in this area? If you find you are weak in this regard, what can you do to improve your time management?

4. Sometimes the pain of yesterday impedes us from living fully today. Can you identify anything from your past that is currently hindering you? What can you do to free yourself from these chains and cease being a prisoner of your past?

5. What do you believe are some of the dangers in not choosing to maximize the time we are given each day? Do you find yourself falling victim to these things? What can you do, what immediate changes can you make, in order to make the most of the time you have available?

Legacy 101

Course Description

No one can cheat fate. Try though some may to postpone or outrun it, ultimately death takes us all. The memory of who we were does not have to end with our physical passing, however. There have lived and died men and women who now belong to the ages because they established legacies that could not be erased. Each and every one of us has the ability to do the same.

Your legacy will be shaped by what you endure, by what you sacrifice, by what you create. Your impact and influence on the generations to follow will be measured by your words and deeds today. If you choose to live in obscurity, your memory will quickly fade into the same. If, however, you choose to strive for greatness, your mark upon this world may be remembered eternally. Will you resolve to live your life so that your name is inscribed upon the hearts and minds of others—even those you have never met—or will you allow it to simply be etched upon a headstone, lost in a sea of anonymity?

One of the most frequently asked questions regarding those who have made a difference in our lives is, "If you could have dinner with any five people, living or dead, who would they be?" My brother and I have discussed this time and time again, and we believe our answer would be Abraham Lincoln, Albert Einstein, Jackie Robinson, Martin Luther King Jr., and Michael Jordan. Why these five individuals? They are all men of destiny. Four of them made their marks and have since moved on; one is still finalizing just how great his impact on the world will be. Although these men come from different eras in history and differ in countless ways, the common trait uniting them all is the lasting impression of the legacies of each left behind.

These five men are no different than my brother and I, no different than you. They took advantage of the opportunities they were granted and made the most of them. They faced challenges and overcame them, persevering in the face of naysayers and those who would steal their dreams. They faced failure but did not give up, believing instead in the purposes established in their hearts. They lived by their own personal creeds and were defined by the habits they established. Each of them had true friends and family members who stood alongside them on their road to their destiny. They understood the blessing inherent in gaining knowledge, but even more importantly they understood the value of applying wisdom in order to grow beyond the mistakes of their pasts. These men knew what they were destined to achieve, even if they displayed this humbly, and they maximized their time refining their gifts and talents in order to release the greatness within them. In short, they all lived according to the lessons we have outlined throughout this book.

In the film Braveheart, William Wallace says, "Every man dies, but not every man really lives." Because these five men truly lived, they will never be forgotten. Because of their accomplishments, they remain immortal through our memories of them. Who is to say that you cannot do the same?

Do you ever wonder how you will be remembered or how your eulogy will read when your time on earth has finally come to an end? Will the lives of those around be improved by your existence?

"Before I became a principal myself, I worked under several others. Some were good, some were mediocre, and some were simply bad. I still learned

something from each one, however. I took mental notes on everything I observed because I knew I would be a principal myself one day.

"As we discuss the topic of legacy, one of my former supervisors deserves special mention, although not in a positive way. She ran the school like it was her personal empire; she reigned as dictator while everyone else served as her minions. She was so mean, she made pit bulls whimper. Needless to say she wasn't well-liked. 'Vibe-killer,' 'killjoy,' and 'wet blanket' were names we attributed to her.

"I still remember the first day she was absent. I walked into the front office, and the room almost seemed to glow from all the smiles. 'What's going on?' I asked. 'She's not here,' one of the secretaries responded, motioning towards the principal's office. 'All day?' I asked. 'Not coming in at all,' the secretary said, beaming from ear to ear. 'Going to be a good day,' a teacher said as she walked back to her room. That day I remember thinking about how sad it would be to live a life where people celebrated my absence instead of being saddened that I was not there to make the environment a more positive one.

"I knew that one day I would have the opportunity to head my own school. I also knew that when that day came, I would lead in such a manner that people would cry when I wasn't around. And so it was. When I resigned from Centerville Elementary in 2014 to pursue my dream of becoming a writer, I went and personally said goodbye to every teacher. One of them looked at me and said, 'I'm going to cry, Mr. Cristales.'

"My final goodbye was to my secretary, a person I loved and continue loving to this day. We hugged, refusing to let go until the tears had subsided. I walked

away satisfied, knowing that I had left some good memories there. In the end that's all we really are—memories—so we should ensure that we do everything possible to be a good one."

- Axel Cristales

At a young age, right around the time when we started questioning our place in this world, my brother and I made a conscious decision to go after our dreams regardless of the cost. Not surprisingly, this coincided with the season in our lives when our dad abandoned us, leaving our mom alone to serve as both parents to her two young boys. Our mom was paying a heavy price at the time to keep us clothed and fed. In doing so, she not only became the ultimate caregiver, but also cemented her own legacy for those that knew her.

As Ralph Stockman, senior pastor of Christ Church in New York, once wrote, "What makes greatness is starting something that lives after you." To us, our mother will always be the great woman who built two great men. Her greatness has been embedded in us. Even after she is gone, her legacy will forever live on through us, through our children, and through our children's children. We continue the path paved by our mother, as will our descendants, persisting even when resistance arises.

Our mother was the original trailblazer for us. Now we have accepted that mantle. We are the trailblazers and, as such, cannot and will not take shortcuts. We seek out opportunities and embrace challenges. We do not see boundaries, but rather break through them because this is what our mother taught us to do. Like her, we want to establish a legacy that leaves a lasting impact, one that will be remembered for generations. When all is said and done, we want others to say, "Nothing was impossible for them. Impossible was not even in their vocabulary." Through our words and deeds, we want to make the lives of others better. About us, the Cristales brothers, we want it to be said, "They cared; they forgave; they loved; they helped; they motivated; they empowered."

"Throughout this book, I've shared a great deal about my experiences growing up, particularly as they relate to my family. In reading our words, it may

seem that we still hold a bit of resentment toward our father. Nothing could be further from the truth, however. I cannot tell you the exact date, nor can I recall the exact moment I did so, but I made a decision to forgive our father for his actions, as did my brother. Nothing special occurred to bring about this change. I just decided that I could not live with bitterness and resentment anymore. That does not mean, however, that my decision to forgive was not put to the test.

"This took place in September of 2004 at my grandmother's funeral, my father's mother. It had been years since my father had seen us, and I honestly did not know what to expect when he did. Not only had it been years since we had seen our father, it had also been years since we really interacted with my dad's side of the family. As it has been said by many people, however, death has a way of uniting a family that has been estranged.

"I could feel my father's eyes on Axel and me as family members and loved ones reflected on the life of my grandmother the night of the viewing service. Even more eyes were on us after the viewing, when people were gathering in the fellowship hall because that is when my father walked up to me and my brother and apologized. We could have ignored his apology, but we didn't. Instead, we listened to what he had to say.

"He talked about how sorry he was, about how he let us down and how he wished he would have been there for us. Our response was to tell him, 'Dad, it's okay. We made it in spite of everything that went down when we were little, and we forgive you. There is your chance right there to do things right this time,' we said as we pointed to his two younger kids.

"As Martin Luther King Jr. said, 'Forgiveness is not an occasional act, it is a constant attitude.' Little did I know that the decision to forgive my father was going to enhance the legacy I am leaving. One of the most significant examples of how regards what took place on April 11, 2009.

""I will never forget that date. It marks the day my beautiful daughter was born. She was born on a cold, spring afternoon at 3:33 p.m. in Room 3. There's something very significant about that. In the Christian faith, the number three symbolizes the Holy Trinity—God the Father, God the Son, God the Spirit—and represents wholeness and Divine perfection. I am not here to get into a theological debate as I am neither a theologian nor somebody who has even attended a Bible school, but I am someone who lives by three attributes that are said in the Bible to be supreme above all others: faith, hope, and love.

On that cold April day, the number three was in full swing as I held my daughter in my arms for the first time.

"That experience convinced me more than ever that God truly does exist. As I gazed into my daughter's eyes, her loud cries didn't bother me at all because I saw all the opportunities and possibilities that awaited her, and I knew I could and would help her achieve them. Her middle name is Grace, and I can honestly say that she became my little saving grace at that moment. In that instant, she put many things into perspective for me. In fact, everyday since she's been born she's been doing that without even knowing it.

"How has she done this? Well, as I stayed with her and her mother in the hospital room, I was confronted with a choice. I had to decide whether or not to call my father and inform him that he was now a grandparent to his third grandchild. I wrestled with making the call, not because I was furious with my dad, but rather because of our past. Although our relationship had been restored at that point, it was still difficult for us to function as father and son. In fact, he will tell you that we're more like friends. Weeks and sometimes months pass by without either of us hearing anything from the other. However, that was no ordinary moment. That was a moment of perfect joy and, although I hesitated, I knew I had to inform him of the great news whether he was going to show up or not.

"I am happy to say my father did show up the next day to visit his newest grandchild, and he was thrilled to be there. It brought me joy to see his face light up as he held her. I am sure the way he showered love upon her that day was his chance to shower love upon us the way he had not been able to years before. I had no ill feelings toward him.

What he had done was in the past, and it had helped mold and shape my brother and me into the men we are today. Being bitter would have done more harm to me than it would have done to him. As a clergyman once said, 'Being bitter is like drinking poison and hoping that it kills the other person.' My choices that weekend were either to bring back anger and resentment and pretend my father did not exist and was not worthy enough to see his grandchild, or forgive, let go, and realize he would always live in me and, since he did, he would always live in my daughter's life as well.

"I have never regretted the decision I made that day. It will only bless my little girl . . . and she is the greatest legacy I could ever leave behind."

- A.C. Cristales

One thing my brother and I have learned on our journey is that peace and security are not the same thing. In December of 2013, we made decision to leave our secure careers as public educators and pursue our dreams of becoming a full-time motivational speaker and a full-time fiction writer. For more than ten years, we were comfortable; we were safe. But we were not at peace. We always saw more potential in ourselves than just serving in the public education system. While we loved the children we served, and while we honor the men and women who dedicate their lives to such a noble career, we knew that we were limiting ourselves and cheating the purpose in our hearts. We might have envisioned ourselves as superintendents of school districts one day, perhaps even Commissioners of Education, but pursuing those goals would have meant following the road most travelled. We would not have been writing our own story, but rather joining in the stories of other men and women who had come before us.

Today we hold the pen in our hands, and the story we are writing is already one of triumph for we have already overcome the greatest enemy to success—fear. We may have given up security, but the peace we have obtained in return is of far greater value, the peace that comes in knowing that the adventure we have embarked on will bring us closer to our destinies.

Horace Mann once said, "You ought to be ashamed to die until you have won something for humanity." One day you may find yourself living in abundance. When that day comes remember that the legacy you leave will not be measured by how much you made, but rather by how much you gave. True success will only exist if there is a successor to your name and true wealth will be determined by your influence upon the hearts of the people who followed you.

"One of the greatest material possessions I have is a framed picture of my son right before he turned one with the poem below framed next to it. I keep it in my office and look at it every day. I let it to speak to me and remind me why I do what I do, remind me that the legacy I leave behind is not just for me, but for my son and daughter as well.

To Any Little Boy's Father

There are little eyes upon you and
they're watching night and day;
There are little ears that quickly take in
everything you say.
There are little hands all eager to do
everything you do.
And a little boy who is dreaming of the
day he will be like you.
You're the little fellow's idol. You're the
wisest of the wise.
In his little mind about you no
suspicions ever rise.
He believes in you devoutly, holds all
that you say and do.
He will say and do in your way when he's
grown up just like you.
There's a wide-eyed little fellow who
believes you're always right.
And his ears are always open and he
watches day and night.
You are setting an example every day in
all you do.
For the little boy who is waiting to grow
up to be like you.

Just how significant your legacy will be will be determined by how you live your life from this moment forward, by what you leave behind once you are no longer here. In your hands you hold a ball of clay that you are shaping by your actions, by how you live your life. In a very real sense destiny is in your hands. You are the potter. What will you create?

As my brother and I pen these final words in this, the final course of our book, we would like to remind you that your life is like a book as well, the pages of which will one day be flipped through and read. Our hope is that you live a life that writes a story worthy of being considered a classic.

Be remembered. Be immortal. Leave a legacy that touches others and makes a difference in the lives of men and women the world over. Your destiny is in your hands. You *can* make this a reality. All it will require is the conscious decision to do so.

What will your decision be?

Legacy 101
Questions for Reflection

1. If you were planning a dinner and could invite five guests, living or dead, from any era of history to dine with you, who would you select? Why would you choose these five individuals above all others?

2. If our legacy is determined by the choices we make, what are some things you can do to ensure the choices you make from this point forward will leave a legacy that inspired those around you?

3. Do you think that if you never pursue your dream or goal, your legacy will be all it was supposed to be? Why or why not?

4. When you have breathed your last breath on this earth, how do you want to be remembered?

5. In ten words or less, what would you want written on your tombstone?

Commencement

Congratulations!

It is with great pleasure that we celebrate your completion of this book and what we hope will be your initiation into a better life. You are now in a moment of transition, with the opportunity to reassess your past, evaluate your present, and begin creating a brighter future no matter how unimaginable it may still seem. As is true with any ending, you now face the challenge of a new beginning. We believe your future is full of endless opportunities, opportunities to make the world a better place not only for yourself, but also for others around you. With faith, hope and love, you *can* see this goal realized.

Though the future is uncertain, do not be afraid. Change is inevitable; progress is avoidable. All roads lead somewhere, and no road is longer or more winding than the road of success. If you choose to travel this path, take heart and be strengthened by what you have already accomplished in life. The education you received long before you picked up this book has been well-earned and can serve as the foundation for deeper wisdom. We sincerely believe that the ten lessons we have shared will grant you freedom to reap the benefits of this, as well as enjoy the success you long for, the success you deserve.

Before any change can occur around you, change must first occur within you. The course of your life and how far you travel upon it begins and ends with how you view yourself. Believe in who you are destined to be and what you are destined to do; believe in the God-given gifts and talents that will assist you in seeing your destiny fulfilled. The impact you will have on this world depends on how brightly you allow the light inside of you to burn. We urge you to let it outshine the sun.

Every lesson we have related, every story we have shared, every word we have written have had but one purpose—to provide you with a vision. As the Proverbs 29:18 says, "Where there is no vision, the people perish." We do not want you to waste away in life, but to thrive. Whatever dream you have, whatever goals you have set, you must grant yourself the power to achieve them by being willing to look beyond your shortcomings, your mistakes, and your failures and focus instead upon the possibilities still before you. The new has come; the old has passed away.

Throughout these courses we have endeavored to nourish your faith, hope, and love. We hope that we have motivated you with our words and provided you with the inspiration to move forward toward your dreams as we have, to open your mind to new possibilities and your heart to a whole new world. Before you close this book, we encourage you to consider the myriad opportunities that lie before you right this moment. While you may not be certain of what the future may bring, do not doubt the greatness that lies within you. You have the ability to respond to any challenges and to overcome all opposition with grace and wisdom, come what may. Now, set out to do so. Leave a legacy that cannot be ignored.

We cannot express how excited we are that you chose to spend time with us. Thank you. Once again, congratulations. May God bless you and all those whose lives you touch.

Eternal 3.

A.C. and Axel Cristales

Made in the USA
San Bernardino, CA
13 August 2014